M000200196

STRATEGIC
PAUSE

STRATEGIC PAUSE

Stop. Think. Lead.

DON GRAUMANN

Copyright © 2020 Donald Graumann. All rights reserved.

No part of this publication may be reproduced, distributed, stored in or introduced into a retrieval system, or transmitted in any form or by any means, including photocopying, recording, or other electronic or mechanical methods, without the prior written permission of the publisher or author, except in the case of brief quotations embodied in reviews, and certain other non-commercial uses permitted by copyright law.

Limit of Liability/Disclaimer of Warranty: While the publisher and author have used their best efforts in preparing this book, they make no representations or warranties with respect to the accuracy or completeness of the contents of this book and specifically disclaim any implied warranties of merchantability or fitness for a particular purpose. No warranty may be created or extended by sales representatives or written sales materials. The advice and strategies contained herein may not be suitable for your situation. You should consult with a professional where appropriate. Neither the publisher not the author shall be liable for damages arising herefrom.

Author:	Don Graumann
Title:	Strategic Pause: Stop. Think. Lead.
	First Edition
Publisher:	Strategic Pause, Don.Graumann@StrategicPause.com
Editor:	Robin Gullicksen, robinredpen@gmail.com
Cover Design:	OneDesigns, info.onedesigns@gmail.com
Interior Design:	Open Heart Designs, jamie@openheartdesigns.com
Subjects:	Leadership, Management, Leadership Development, Career Development, Self-help, Personal Growth, Success

ISBN: 978-1-7356152-0-2 (eBook)
ISBN: 978-1-7356152-1-9 (Hardcover)
ISBN: 978-1-7356152-2-6 (Paperback)

To the GCOM & AMEX Programming Groups,
the GMNA Team, the ATEC Account Group, the ATLAS Team,
the FSI Vertical, and my Leadership Coachees,

I have learned so much from you. More than you know.
You helped write this book. I am honored to
have been called your Leader.

Read Don's Leadership Blog

http://StrategicPause.com

-or-

https://www.linkedin.com/in/dongraumann/detail/recent-activity/posts/

Follow Don on LinkedIn

https://www.linkedin.com/in/dongraumann/

Follow Don on twitter

@DonThinks

Contents

PREFACE XIII

PART 1: INTRODUCTION   1

1.1 WHY DID I WRITE THIS BOOK? 3
1.2 WHAT IS A STRATEGIC PAUSE? 4
1.3 WHAT IS A PERSONAL LEADERSHIP MODEL? 5
    Explicit, Simple, Actionable (ESA Qualities)...............................5
    Not Just Best Practices..6
1.4 WHO NEEDS A PERSONAL LEADERSHIP MODEL? 7
1.5 WHY DO YOU NEED A PERSONAL LEADERSHIP MODEL? 9
    "Know how you impact the big picture." 9
    Growth & Sustainable Results 9
    Followers & Leaders 10
1.6 WHY SHOULD YOU LISTEN TO ME? 11
    Sustained Results 11
    My Leadership Journey 14
1.7 HOW DO YOU BUILD A PERSONAL LEADERSHIP MODEL? 18
    Principles and Methods..18
    Make It Your Own..19
    Classroom Leadership Evolution...20
    Leadership is a Process, Not a Destination...............................23
    Transforming Gray into Black and White 24
1.8 HOW SHOULD YOU USE THIS BOOK?..........................25
    Book Layout...25
    Reading Process 27
1.9 HOW DO YOU GET STARTED? 29

2.1 YOUR BEHAVIORAL MODEL 33

2.2 SITUATION MANAGEMENT 34

Situation Management in my Childhood (Leadership Example) 35

The Unsent Angry Email (Leadership Example) 36

Situation Management & Composure 36

Staying Composed in a Cube Farm (Leadership Example) 37

Witnessing my Mom's Composure (Leadership Example) 38

2.3 LEADERSHIP TEMPLATES & INITIATIVE 41

ESA Process 42

No Big Thinking Sunday Night & Monday Morning (Leadership Template)... 43

Situation Management & Leadership Templates 44

Efficient Errands (Leadership Example) 44

Can vs. Can't Control (Leadership Template) 45

Know When Good Enough is Good Enough (Leadership Template) 46

Take Initiative & Challenge the BAU 47

Writing My Leadership Book (Leadership Example) 47

The Secure Data Hub & PCI Compliance (Leadership Example) 47

Effective over Efficient (Leadership Template) 48

3.1 LEADERSHIP MODEL EVOLUTION 53

Evolution Scenarios..53

The Skills Pie (Leadership Template) 55

Evolution via Red, Yellow, Green..56

3.2 LEADERSHIP MODEL FRAMEWORK...59

The Grid 60

Roadmap 63

3.3 FOUNDATION 66

3.3.1 CORE VALUES 67

Consistent Expectation Setting (Leadership Template) 69

Core Values Integration 70

Ignoring My Gut and the Project Manager (Leadership Example) 72

How to Be a Good Person (Leadership Template).. 73

3.3.2 PERSONAL ORGANIZATION..75

Build an External Mind 76

Personal Organization System Framework (Leadership Template)...............77

Choose Important over Urgent (Leadership Template) 80

Creating a Win-Win by Reframing Priorities (Leadership Template)...............81
Organized at the Appropriate Level (Leadership Template) 82
Beware of False Obligations (Leadership Template)....................................83
Be Ready 84
Ready for Due Diligence (Leadership Example)...85
Big Automotive Client and Scalable Growth (Leadership Example)..............86
Audit Ready (Leadership Example) 87
The Power of Little Habits 88
Ten-minute Rule (Leadership Template)...88

3.4 PRINCIPLES 91

3.4.1 EMPOWERMENT (E) 92
Maximize Strengths, Minimize Weaknesses 92
Know Your Resets (Leadership Template)..95
Your Point of Diminishing Returns (Leadership Template)...........................96
Debating on Your Home Field (Leadership Example)...................................96
"Do What You Do Best Every Day" 97
A Programmer Should Program (Leadership Example)...............................98
The Account Manager with Sales Skills (Leadership Example)....................99
The Accessible Executive (Leadership Example) 100
Scalability through Empowerment (Leadership Example).........................100
Empowerment Evolution...102
Value Proposition 103
Situational People Management (Leadership Template)...........................104

3.4.2 STRATEGIC ALIGNMENT (SA) 107
Breaking into Identification Services (Leadership Example).......................109
Set Vivid Vision & Objectives 111
The Power of YouTube (Leadership Example)...112
Vivid Vision and Objectives (Leadership Example)....................................113
100% Client Advocacy (Leadership Example)..114
Best Practices + 1 (Leadership Template) 114
Cascade Vision & Objectives 115
Cascade as Lead Measures (Leadership Template)..................................116

3.5 METHODS...120

3.5.1 THE STRATEGIC PAUSE 121
Align to Core & Objectives.. 121
Leverage Minds and Hands (Leadership Template)...................................122
The Efficiency Lunch (Leadership Example) 124
Lead Them to Their Own Conclusion (Leadership Template).....................125
Balance Process and Results (Leadership Template) 126
Strategic Procrastination (Leadership Template) 127

The Strategic Pause and War (Leadership Example)................................ 128
"Know how you impact the big picture." 129

3.5.2 STRATEGIC MANAGEMENT 131
Build a Distributed System 131
Distributed Warfare (Leadership Example) 135
Strategic Management Routines 136
Planning..138
Value Propositions (Leadership Example).................................... 139
Loyalty Objectives and Vision (Leadership Example) 141
Top-down and Bottom-up Strategy (Leadership Template)...................... 143
Trend Progression Strategy (Leadership Template).......................... 144
Management..146
Measurement..154
What is left in the tank? (Leadership Example) 155
Populated Framework *(Strategic Management Artifact)*.......................158
Transactional to Systematic..159
Beware of Compliance (Leadership Template) 160
Rollout by Impact 161
NOT Optional 163

3.6 DIFFERENTIATORS 166

3.6.1 BE A POSITIVE FORCE 167
Enthusiasm, Optimism, Humor 168
View as an Opportunity or a Challenge....................................169
Be a Positive Force and Parenting (Leadership Example) 169
Rising through the Breach (Leadership Example)....................................169

3.6.2 SIMPLIFY.. 171
Syntax & Semantics...172
Min Admin, Max Value 173
Connect Status with Rate of Change (Leadership Template) 175

3.6.3 BE TRANSPARENT.. 176
On Message...176
Manage to One Reality 177
Transparency in Projects (Leadership Template)..............................178
The Delayed Proposal Win (Leadership Example) 179

3.7 ESA AS GUARDRAILS 182

PART 4: LEADERSHIP EVOLUTION   185

4.1 SATISFACTION VIA OVERLAP 187
4.2 ROLE EVOLUTION 189
4.3 REAL-WORLD LEADERSHIP EVOLUTION 195

PART 5: CLOSING THOUGHTS   199

5.1 LEADING IN THE "NEW NORMAL" 201
   Remote Working 201
   Replacing the Watercooler 202
5.2 MAKE IT YOUR OWN 203
5.3 FULFILLING POTENTIAL 204
5.4 ACCELERATING HUMAN EVOLUTION 205

PART 6: ARTIFACTS   207

6.1 THE ESA LEADERSHIP MODEL 208
6.2 STRATEGIC MANAGEMENT 209
6.3 ESA AS GUARDRAILS 210
6.4 REAL-WORLD LEADERSHIP EVOLUTION 211

ACKNOWLEDGMENTS 213

LEADERSHIP TEMPLATE INDEX 215
LEADERSHIP EXAMPLES INDEX 217

ABOUT THE AUTHOR 219

Preface

Leaders are not born. Leaders are made. Leadership is learned.

You may have been born with qualities that are helpful to leadership. But, you still need to understand what those qualities are and how to apply them. You need to learn what leadership is and how to be a leader.

When I got the opportunity to move into management, I attacked my leadership development. I studied most of the well-known leadership books written by the leadership gurus. I tracked down and watched video after video. I earned my MBA and took advantage of every opportunity to attend leadership and management training, and I read about transformative historical leaders to learn about their leadership styles. These sources were filled with qualities and concepts related to leadership that resonated with me, but I was still left fuzzy on how to make leadership real. During my leadership journey, I figured it out.

You make leadership real by building, evolving, and living by a personal leadership model. Your model contains the "what" and the "how" of leadership stated in your own words. It also defines your leadership style, which is the "who" of leadership. Helping you build and evolve your personal leadership model is what this book is about.

Strategic Pause is the leadership book that I was looking for. If I had had this book when I started my leadership journey, it would have accelerated my leadership development. I believe that it will invigorate and accelerate your leadership development.

The bookcase in my office is specifically organized. The bottom shelves hold books I have not read yet. In the middle are history books I have read—especially biographies of significant leaders—and above them, books on leadership, management, economics, and business. The top shelf is special. It holds the books that have had the greatest impact on me. These are books that I have read multiple times; they have helped make me who I am. I often recommend books from my top shelf to others. My goal is that *Strategic Pause* makes it to your top shelf.

PART 1

Introduction

1.1 Why did I write this book?

I began my career as a programmer. I loved it and thought I would be happy doing it my entire career. It was an excellent match to my strengths. Even though I was the youngest programmer in my group, I was trusted with training new programmers. Because I really enjoyed helping my peers ramp up, I started wondering if I should consider management.

Shortly after I started exploring that interest, my manager took a position elsewhere in the company. Brad Emerson, my manager's manager, told me that he felt I had a great deal of potential and asked if I would take the position. I was surprised and flattered. I told him that, although I was definitely interested, I did not think I was ready. I had just begun thinking about the possibility of being a manager and did not know where to start. What he did next had a profound impact on me.

Brad asked me how long I needed to get ready. I replied that I thought I could do it in six months. He then ran the programming group in addition to his full-time job, nearly doubling his workload. Four months later, he asked me if I was ready. Because I had been attacking my management and leadership development (as I mentioned in the *Preface* and will discuss further in *My Leadership Journey* in Part 1.6), I had the confidence to accept the promotion.

Brad's belief in my potential and his personal sacrifice was a powerful lesson. It solidified my personal purpose of wanting to do the same for others. I had always viewed people management—leadership—as sort of a sacred responsibility. Now, I could articulate why I wanted to be a leader. I wanted to help individuals and teams fulfill their potential. That is the purpose of this book. That is why I wrote *Strategic Pause*.

1.2 **What is a Strategic Pause?**

If you strive to lead, you should be taking strategic pauses. It is how you lead in the moment and how you lead in the present. It is how you can lead right now.

Your day is comprised of a series of situations. The direction your day takes is determined by how you respond to each of them. The strategic pause is considering all the alternatives and choosing the best response. This concept is captured by the book's subtitle as "Stop. Think. Lead."

Some situations are filled with emotion. By taking a strategic pause, you respond instead of react. You minimize emotion and stay composed.

Some situations look like business as usual. By taking a strategic pause, you take initiative and challenge the established path. You seek alternatives that are more effective and efficient.

By taking strategic pauses, you better align your behavior to what you do best and what your team does best. You better align yourself and your team to the larger objectives.

The strategic pause is the hub of your personal leadership model. It is how you lead in the moment. We will delve much deeper into the strategic pause in Part 2 of this book.

If your minimum takeaway from this book is learning to incorporate strategic pauses into the situations that make up your day, you will be a better leader.

1.3 What is a Personal Leadership Model?

Your maximum takeaway from this book will be building and evolving your personal leadership model. This is the primary focus of *Strategic Pause*.

A personal leadership model is your "what, how, and who" of leadership. The "what" is your understanding of leadership, the *Principles*. The "how" is the process, the *Methods* you use to make progress toward the "what." These principles and methods apply broadly to your team and organization. The "who" is your leadership style, which I refer to as *Differentiators*. Differentiators are principles and methods that are unique to you.

Your leadership model codifies what leadership is and how you go about making it real.

Explicit, Simple, Actionable (ESA Qualities)

Leadership is attainable. Too many people think leaders are born and not made. They view leadership as intangible: something hard to define but obvious when they see it. It does not need to be this way.

By building and evolving a personal leadership model that includes principles and methods, you make leadership *explicit*, *simple*, and *actionable*. I refer to these as the "ESA Qualities."

- Leadership should be *explicit.* If you strive to lead, you should be building your own leadership model and transparently sharing it with your team. It is your leadership system.

- Leadership is *simple.* Much of the time, leadership is simply doing the things you already know you should be doing but are deprioritizing because you let the daily scramble get in the way.

- Leadership must be *actionable.* Just focusing on the concepts of leadership is not enough. You need to translate those concepts into behaviors and, ultimately, outcomes.

Not Just Best Practices

Most good leaders follow some form of a leadership model. However, it is usually a collection of best practices that they have acquired over the years. They explicitly or implicitly seek to apply one or more of their best practices as situations arise. They lead when presented with an opportunity. With this approach, they must review their inventory of leadership best practices in each new situation. You can do better.

By building an explicit, simple, and actionable leadership model, you will be a better leader when opportunities come to you. You will also be a better leader because you will create opportunities to lead. Your team will see a method to your madness. They will see an explicit, simple, and actionable system.

1.4 Who needs a personal leadership model?

The answer to that question is "everyone."

There are many who think leadership should be natural. They do not think they need a leadership model. Although some people are born with qualities that greatly contribute to leadership, there is a big difference between possessing certain qualities and being perceived as a leader.

If you strive to lead, you should be building and evolving your personal leadership model. Your team must believe you have a plan. You must believe you have a plan. Your leadership model is your plan.

If do not think you need a leadership model, there is a high likelihood that your leadership is incomplete. You may not realize it, but you do have one. It is implicit and it is defined by your behavior. If you have a plan—a leadership model—your leadership will be more complete.

If you think you are not trying to be a leader, you still need a leadership model. At some point you will be in a situation in which you have to—and will even want to—lead. You may be forced to by circumstances (for example, your company), or your passion for something will drive you to want to make a difference. Do not wait for those circumstances to arise. Having an existing leadership model will accelerate and maximize your impact when you hit those leadership challenges.

If you work on a team, you should have a leadership model. Knowing how you prefer to be led requires that you have some understanding of what it takes to be a leader. It will make you a better team member and you will be able to provide meaningful feedback to your team leader.

On an even more basic level, before you can attempt to lead others, you must be able to lead yourself. Your personal leadership model has application on both the team and individual levels. You use it to make decisions and choose your behavior. Thus, there is heavy overlap between your personal leadership model and your personal behavioral model. They are, arguably, one and the same. We will go deeper into personal behavioral models when we go deeper into the strategic pause in Part 2.

1.5 Why do you need a personal leadership model?

Having a personal leadership model makes you a better leader and a better team member. It accelerates your personal leadership development. I define my understanding and the purpose of leadership in three ways.

"Know how you impact the big picture."

If every member of your team knows how they impact the big picture, you are a leader. If you personally can say this, you are practicing self-leadership. It means that you and your team know how your unique skills and experience can be leveraged to make the maximum impact. It means that you and your team understand how you are aligned to the bigger objectives. I believe this statement is powerful. It should be every leader's purpose. As a result, it is the headline, or motto, of my personal leadership model.

Growth & Sustainable Results

If you are impacting the big picture, you are driving growth and delivering sustainable results.

I open my leadership coaching relationships with this question: "If your responsibilities increased/grew tenfold, what would you do?" The answer cannot be "work harder." No one can scale up that much. The answer I hear most often is, "I would have to assess the situation to figure out what needs to be done." Your personal leadership model is the answer to the growth question. Regardless of the scope, if you have a personal leadership model, you have a plan that drives growth. You already know what you need to do now and what you need to do next. You just need to fill in the specifics of the circumstances.

Being focused on sustainable results in addition to growth means building something maintainable and repeatable. It is recognizing that the ends do not justify the means. This is especially true regarding impacts to your team. If you cut corners, you are not building something sustainable and will be tempted to cut corners in the future. When you do things right today, it will be much easier to do them right tomorrow. Your personal leadership model guides you and your team to do the right things and build a system that is maintainable. It powers sustainable results.

Followers & Leaders

You will note that I use the phrase "strive to lead" rather than just "lead." Anyone can declare themselves a leader, but only followers can determine if someone is truly a leader. Going a step further, true leaders strive to build new leaders in addition to earning followers. By developing others as leaders, dependence on your individual contribution decreases significantly, and the probability that your team will deliver sustainable results increases dramatically. Although "Followers & Leaders" could easily be included in "Sustainable Results," the point about building new leaders deserves reinforcement.

1.6 Why should you listen to me?

I hope what I have shared so far is resonating with you. But why should you listen to me? Why am I a credible leadership expert and coach? I can answer that question in two ways.

Sustained Results

Living by my personal leadership model has helped my teams deliver sustained results.

I have been evolving and striving to lead by my leadership model for 25 years. It has evolved quite a bit and has had different names, but many of the foundational principles and methods have been there in some form from the start.

Over the 25 years, I have held five roles in which I lived by my leadership model:

- Programming Manager, general commercial division
- Technical Director/Account Leader, large automotive account
- Account Group Vice President, accounts in multiple industries
- General Manager, major financial services account
- Division Leader, 35 financial services and insurance accounts

In 21 of those years, I have been able to capture data related to leadership impact.

I acknowledge that many inputs have factored into the successes I cite. Whenever possible, I have compared my team metrics to those of the larger company's to nullify inputs such as industry tailwinds, etc. As a result, I am confident that my leadership model was a meaningful driver of sustained results.

Growth

I measure success for growth based on whether my account, group, or division exceeded its growth target. I have 21 years of data. We exceeded the target in 14 of those 21 years (67%). I think virtually any business manager would be proud of a 67% success rate on growth targets.

Margin/Profitability

I measure success for margin based on whether my account, group, or division exceeded the margin target. I have 21 years of data. We exceeded the target in 19 of 21 years (90%). In 12 of those years (60%), margin improved year over year.

I am immensely proud of these results. To me, this represents doing things the right way. It is the sustainable part of sustainable results. Note that these profitability results were not achieved by cutting human capital costs. They were the results of continuous improvement and innovation.

Quality

Measuring quality is not as straightforward as measuring growth and margin. For quality, I combine annual metrics for satisfactory client-facing scorecards and reduction of client-facing incidents year to year. I have 16 years of data for quality. We met or exceeded our objectives in 13 of those years (81%).

Similar to margin, maintaining and improving quality speaks to doing things the right way.

Associate Attrition

Attrition is a clear indicator of effective leadership and it is an important metric. During the 21 years, I measured my team's attrition against the larger company's four times. In all four instances, it was dramatically lower (4/4 = 100%). Our attrition range was 6–8% in the periods of measurement compared to the larger company's attrition range of 16–22%.

Another anecdotal measure is "boomerang rate." This is when someone who left the team for another internal team, or left the company altogether, seeks to return to the team. I do not have hard metrics for boomerang rate. However, I can cite multiple HR and recruiting leader statements noting associate desire to return to my team. To me, this is the highest form of advocacy.

Engagement

The results I have covered so far are lagging metrics that are all tied to the leading metric of engagement. Like attrition, associate engagement is a measure of management and leadership effectiveness. I have 9 years of engagement data. In all 9 years, my team's engagement was significantly higher than that of the larger company's (9/9 = 100%). My team often scored 25–50% higher, depending on the metric.

Confidence

The final sustained result of confidence is difficult to quantify, but I have found it to be a tremendous benefit. When you strive to lead, your team can sense if you believe in the direction you are setting and the manner in which you move forward. If they think you believe, they are more likely to believe and to follow.

If you have a personal leadership model, you have a plan. You are not at the whim of each situation you encounter. Your model's principles and methods drive your behavior. Instead of fully evaluating every situation individually to determine your point of view, you can frame them in terms of your leadership model. If you are asked why you have made a particular decision, you can cite your internalized and independent foundation. With this process, you become more predictable to your team and to others around you. Having a clear approach helps you build self-confidence and helps build your team's confidence in you.

My Leadership Journey

I have been an eager and willing student of leadership since the late 1990s. You could say that I have turned over every rock I could find on the subject. Once I decided to learn how to lead, how did I go about it?

I was a math major in college. In math, there are three foundational properties: commutative, distributive, and associative. They apply to algebra, functions, matrices, vectors, etc. In observing my peers, I found it strange that they would spend time studying these properties whenever we started a new field. To me, the properties were the properties; their application was obvious regardless of the field.

When I graduated from college and started my first job as a programmer, I knew Pascal, Lisp, and some assembly language. I thought knowing the syntax of these programming languages made me a programmer. Over a few years, I learned FORTRAN, then SAS, then FoxPro, then C, then C++, and then C#. Like the foundational properties of math, I saw commonalities across the programming languages. I quickly realized that being a programmer was not knowing the syntax of a specific language. Being a programmer was knowing how to design and build logic; it was knowing the principles and methods of solid programming. Once I compiled my version of those principles and methods, the language I was programming in did not matter. For example, I just needed to decide if the requirements called for an iterative or conditional looping structure. Once I made that decision, I could look up the specific syntax from the programming language's reference manual. It was at this point that the concept of "syntax and semantics" really set in. I explicitly strove to translate syntax into semantics with the goal of isolating the underlying principle or method so I could apply it more broadly.

When I got the opportunity to manage my programming group, I knew exactly what I needed to do. Focusing on semantics over syntax had enabled me to become a stronger programmer. In my mind, moving into management would be no different. So, I set about learning the semantics of management and leadership.

My study of leadership started with the well-known leadership books. If it was a notable work, I read and studied it. I created a leadership cheat sheet similar to what I pulled together for my principles and methods of solid programming. This collection of management and leadership best practices was my first personal leadership model.

After reading every book and article on leadership that I could get my hands on, I started to notice common themes. If a topic was reinforced by multiple sources, I concluded that it must be foundational and thus must be included in my leadership model. In this manner, I accumulated a collection of management and leadership conceptual frameworks. Some directly informed my personal leadership model, which was a conceptual framework itself. Others that I deemed not quite as important, I kept in my inventory in case they could be useful in the future. I call these conceptual frameworks "leadership templates," which we will cover in Part 2 and reference throughout the book.

Next, I focused on learning about impactful leaders. I devoured books on U.S. presidents, generals, transformative social leaders, and others. Studying these influential people reinforced the themes captured from the leadership books and highlighted the positive impact that certain personal qualities have on leadership. As with the leadership books, I started to see many overlapping themes. I found that many notable figures, such as Elon Musk and Peter Thiel, cite "first principles" as critical to their approach to innovation, strategy, and leadership. You will find first principles in philosophy, mathematics, and physics. It is the concept of starting with and building on the elements that cannot be simplified any further. For our purposes, it is the same as syntax and semantics. This was confirmation that I was on the right track.

At the same time, I was also observing my environment. I watched everyone around me, especially those in management and leadership roles. I learned a ton, probably more about what not to do than what to do. It was also during this time that I started to write in a journal. I found it to be extremely valuable as I worked on evolving my leadership model.

Knowing there were aspects of business that a technical manager like myself was not being exposed to, I decided to pursue an MBA. It was eye opening and it greatly deepened my business acumen. But one insight was transformational. I still viewed myself as a programmer who had worked my way into management. I assumed that my career path was moving toward a CTO position. I thought that because I was technical, I could not be strategic. Business school changed all that. Strategy, without a doubt, was within my grasp. In fact, I came to believe that my "nerd" (technical) background, which drove me to build an explicit and simple leadership model, was a critical advantage.

Since earning my MBA, I have continued to grow as a leader. I have shared my leadership model with every one of my teams, and I have attempted to apply it to broader and broader responsibilities. On each of the levels described previously, it has helped deliver sustainable results.

I also view leadership coaching on an individual level as essential to my growth. Coaching helps individuals grow as leaders while helping me fine tune my leadership model. Our discussions consistently uncover wrinkles and aspects of leadership that are new to me. I continue to coach people on leadership and personal productivity in both their professional and personal lives.

1.7 How do you build a personal leadership model?

My personal leadership model has evolved over 25 years. It works. It is called the "ESA Leadership Model" because the two primary principles are *Empowerment* and *Sustainable Advantage*, which we will cover in depth in *Principles* (Part 3.4).

Throughout the book, you will see "ESA" applied in three ways. In *What is a Personal Leadership Model* (Part 1.3), you learned about ESA qualities. Explicit, simple, and actionable are qualities that a leadership model should have. Later, in *Leadership Templates & Initiative* (Part 2.2), you will learn about the ESA process: be explicit, simplify, and make it actionable. You use this process to understand and simplify new insights into what I call *leadership templates*, which you can then leverage in your decision-making and potentially integrate into your personal leadership model. I will refer to these two applications specifically as ESA qualities and the ESA process. When used alone, "ESA" will refer to the ESA leadership model itself. It is the most important application of ESA.

Learning about all aspects of ESA will help you build and evolve your own personal leadership model. If you are just beginning your leadership journey, it will be your starting point. If you are an experienced leader and already have a leadership model, I am certain that comparing it with ESA will strengthen your existing model.

Principles and Methods

As mentioned in *What is a Personal Leadership Model* (Part 1.3), a personal leadership model is composed of principles and methods.

The principles are the "what." They could be any concept such as a value, quality, or idea. The methods are the "how." They are the processes or behaviors that advance the principles. Methods make the principles real. Emphasizing methods along with principles makes this leadership development book actionable.

Make It Your Own

In *Strategic Pause*, I walk through my personal leadership model. If you choose to accept it verbatim, you will be executing my model. While you will get results, they will be less sustainable. You need to make it your own. I want you to put your model in your own words. Where it makes sense, I want you to swap in or add principles and methods that have greater meaning to you. To facilitate this, there are intentional gaps. While I provide my perspective, it is up to you to fill in the gaps. Look at my leadership model as guardrails. This approach will maximize your internalization of the principles and methods, and the result will be your own personal leadership model.

Some components are **mandatory**. Any leadership model would be incomplete without them. These mandatory principles and methods, however, should be translated into your own words.

Some components are **highly suggested**. You must have a good reason for swapping them out. I suggest that you also put these principles and methods in your own words.

Finally, some components are **personalized**. You can choose to put what I share in your own words. However, I believe you will discover other principles or methods specific to you that you should swap for mine.

Please note that I did not invent leadership models, nor did I invent all of the concepts contained within my leadership model. I learned about them from other sources and made them my own.

Classroom Leadership Evolution

In controlled conditions, you would learn about the ESA leadership model and build your personal leadership model in the order I lay out below. I call it "Classroom Leadership Evolution." It is a preview of the order in which the primary content in this book is presented: *The Strategic Pause* (Part 2) and *The ESA Leadership Model* (Part 3). This is the most logical way to build a personal leadership model.

In the real world, however, your leadership evolution will take a different path. The real world is messy. Oftentimes, you will learn about a principle or method after you need it. You learn by trial and error. I lay out the real-world order in *Real-world Leadership Evolution* (Part 4.3). By structuring this book around the "Classroom Leadership Evolution" order instead, I am striving to prepare you for situations at every level of leadership before they arise.

The five high-level steps below represent "Classroom Leadership Evolution" and the general outline of *Strategic Pause*:

1. **THE STRATEGIC PAUSE:** Practicing strategic pauses is how you lead in the moment. It is how you can start leading right now. It is putting this book's subtitle into action: "Stop. Think. Lead." The strategic pause has three levels that represent going deeper into "Think" and "Lead." We will cover levels one and two in *The Strategic Pause* (Part 2) and level three in *Methods* (Part 3.5). The strategic pause is the hub of your larger leadership model and critical to applying your model's other principles and methods. The strategic pause is mandatory.

2. **LEADERSHIP TEMPLATES:** Leadership templates are conceptual models that you use to understand, simplify, and apply new concepts. The Golden Rule and the strategic pause are examples. You will leverage leadership templates to flush out alternative

responses and better inform your decision-making. We will go deeper into these conceptual models in *Leadership Templates & Initiative* (Part 2.2).

Your larger personal leadership model is a collection of leadership templates. As you learn a new one, assess it relative to your model to determine if it should be included. We address this integration process in *Leadership Model Evolution* (Part 3.1). Throughout this book, I share leadership templates that will inform your strategic pauses and may contribute to your personal leadership model. Leadership templates are personalized. You need to create them in your own words as you encounter new principles and methods.

3. **THE ESA LEADERSHIP MODEL FRAMEWORK:** To have a complete leadership model, what must it include? The leadership model framework answers that question. For example, every leadership model framework must cover how to manage people and build teams. Over the years, I have evolved my framework so that it covers the bases of leadership. We go much deeper into the topic in *Leadership Model Framework* (Part 3.2).

The ESA Leadership Model Framework is highly suggested. It is how your leadership model is organized. From earlier in the introduction, you know that it has slots for principles and methods. At the very least, your framework must include both of these. Note that the framework itself is a leadership template.

4. **THE ESA LEADERSHIP MODEL:** This is my personal leadership model. It is my leadership model framework filled in with principles and methods. Building on the example above, sharing

the principle of empowerment and outlining routines like meaningful one-on-ones, which we will cover in *Empowerment* (Part 3.4.1) and *Strategic Management* (Part 3.5.2), are central to my approach to managing people and building teams. We will walk through ESA in four sections:

▸▸ **Foundation**: *Core Values* and *Personal Organization* underlie the rest of your personal leadership model. They have significant bearing on the impact of the other principles and methods. Having core values and a personal organization system is mandatory. The form they take is personalized. We will cover these in *Foundation* (Part 3.3).

▸▸ **Principles**: *Empowerment* and *Strategic Alignment* are the primary principles of ESA. It is why the model is named "ESA." Empowerment is isolating and leveraging core strengths and value propositions, which are your tools. Strategic alignment is setting the destination and aligning the team and offering accordingly. The ESA principles are highly suggested. That said, my experience is that the majority of personal leadership models will include these principles. We will cover this in *Principles* (Part 3.4)

▸▸ **Methods**: *The Strategic Pause* and *Strategic Management* are the primary methods of ESA. The strategic pause helps you lead in the present. Strategic management is putting a system of management routines in place that represents leadership in the future. The strategic pause is mandatory. Putting strategic management in place is also mandatory, though the actual form is personalized. We will cover these in *Methods* (Part 3.5).

▸ *Differentiators*: This is your leadership style. It is isolating your core strengths, specific innate principles and methods that apply to leadership. More than anywhere else in your personal leadership model, this is where you make it your own. Differentiators are personalized. We will cover them in *Differentiators* (Part 3.6).

5. **EVOLVE**: Building and evolving your personal leadership model, like leadership, is not a linear path. It is a cycle. You are always taking strategic pauses. You are responding to individual situations as well as building out and executing strategic management. You are encountering new leadership templates and considering how they may improve your overall leadership model. You are not only adding and building; you are also simplifying and contracting. If your leadership model becomes too big and complicated, it will be less actionable. Do not hesitate to leave leadership templates behind. While the concepts they capture may be valuable, the templates not integrated into your model are less important than your leadership model overall.

Leadership is a Process, Not a Destination

Taking a class on leadership will not make you a leader. Only your behavior and performance over time will result in you being viewed as a leader. Training and seminars can improve skills and change perspectives, but your actions make you a leader.

Further, if you strive to lead, this learning and evolution is continuous. You will fine tune your leadership model based on introspection and circumstances. Over time, you will cover the same ground, challenge legacy components, and make new observations. That said, you will find that many core components stay consistent.

As stated earlier, the steps described above are the high-level outline of *The Strategic Pause* (Part 2) and *The ESA Leadership Model* (Part 3). This is the most logical path to build a personal leadership model.

Transforming Gray into Black and White

One benefit of your leadership model evolution is that you will find yourself less influenced by the latest management/leadership fads. We all know peers and team members who get excited about the latest buzz and want to make a change to the operating model as a result. In my experience, the majority of management fads are just a repackaging of age-old leadership, solid management, and personal productivity wisdom. If you are committed to living by your personal leadership model, you will be better able to simplify the latest fad into terms—a leadership template—that are either already a part of your model or terms that you have already considered and set aside.

Beyond being able to quickly assess management fads, having a personal leadership model enables you to digest the broader world more quickly. Many people see the world around them as mostly gray. If a situation is gray, you try to figure out what is going on and determine your perspective. When you have foundational principles and methods guiding your thinking and decisions, things become significantly less gray. It becomes easier and easier to frame gray situations as black and white based on your principles and methods. This is particularly true of one's core values, which we will discuss in *Foundation* (Part 3.3). Even more generally, if you explicitly know what you believe, you can reach a conclusion about a new situation far more quickly than if you do not know what you believe. Having a personal leadership model means you are better able to transform a gray situation into black and white so you can make an informed decision.

1.8 How should you use this book?

Setting clear expectations is a particularly important skill, especially when you are striving to lead. As a result, I want to set clear expectations on how to use this book.

Book Layout

The focus of this book is to help you build and evolve your personal leadership model. As you know, your leadership model should be explicit, simple, and actionable. For this reason, I have tried to make this book's format explicit, simple, and actionable.

Concise

I want you to use *Strategic Pause*. I want you to read and internalize what I have shared. As a result, my goal was to keep it short, though I could easily have written 500 pages. I have tried to keep each concept to no more than five points.

I do not cover much of the research behind the knowledge I share. If it is in ESA, I have seen it work firsthand or studied the science behind the insight and its application. As particular concepts resonate with you, I recommend that you go deeper. Further interest and research will help you with the articulation to make it your own. For the purposes of this book, I have kept it simple to keep you moving forward.

Flow

You can read *Strategic Pause* cover to cover. That is the order I recommend. However, I chose to write it in a modular format so that it may be read in virtually any order. Each chapter and section, for the most part, can stand alone.

In *Leadership Evolution* (Part 4), I have listed alternative mappings of the book's content. For example, you will find typical career milestones listed along with the chapters most relevant to their development in *Role Evolution* (Part 4.2).

Chapter Format

Each chapter has no more than four types of content. I did my best to be consistent throughout.

1. **PRIMARY CONTENT:** This is the principle or method that I am sharing. It is the lesson. The content will frequently refer to a "leadership artifact" that we will build out. A leadership artifact is simply the visual representation of all or part the ESA leadership model.

2. **LEADERSHIP EXAMPLES:** Where applicable, I will share from one to three examples of the primary content. Think of them as mini case studies. I have tried to keep them as simple as possible. Leadership examples are denoted with growth arrows:

3. **LEADERSHIP TEMPLATES:** You will learn much more about leadership templates in *Leadership Templates & Initiative* (Part 2.2). They are conceptual models that you can use to guide your behavior and decisions. Where appropriate, I will share leadership templates related to the primary content. Leadership templates are denoted with a pause button:

4. **THINKING QUESTIONS:** I will suggest relevant questions for you to think about. These will help you understand and internalize the principles and methods covered in the primary content. They will help you make it your own. Thinking questions are denoted by fast-forward bullets:

Reading Process

Strategic Pause is not meant to be read cover to cover in only a few sittings. It should accompany you as you build and evolve your personal leadership model over time. It is intended to accelerate the process and your overall development as a leader. As a result, you should read it as though it were a textbook: one that you can refer to often.

Read, Internalize, Repeat

I recommend that you read this book in intervals of five to ten minutes and then think about and internalize the concepts. I envision you reading one or two chapters and then starting your commute, walking the dog, going for a run, taking a shower, waiting for your flight to board, or doing any other activity where you have time to think. Use the *Thinking Questions* to help you during these activities.

Partner with a Journal

I am a strong believer in journaling. I have been journaling since 1999 and am currently on #41. I have found that journaling helps me consider and internalize new concepts. It has been extremely valuable in my leadership development.

I call my journal a "Think Book." I bet you can see where I am going. I focus my journal on "meaningful thoughts" rather than writing about the mundane or the day-to-day. When I have a meaningful thought or observation—especially on the topics of leadership or personal productivity—I record a voice memo on my phone or, if I am in a situation where I should not speak, I send myself a shorthand email. When I sit down to journal, I have topics ready to think and write about. Early mornings and during flights are excellent times to think and write in your journal.

The Network Effect

My greatest hope is that this book will have such a positive impact on you that you proactively share its principles and methods. The vivid picture that comes to mind is of someone sharing a challenge or a desire to grow in some way. I envision you jumping to the whiteboard or pulling out a scrap of paper to share your personal leadership model, which was the result of you taking ESA and making it your own. As the enthusiastic discussion unfolds, you ultimately recommend reading *Strategic Pause*. Maybe you even have a copy on hand to show and share!

1.9 How do you get started?

Hopefully, your next question is, "How do I get started?" More specifically, "How do I begin my classroom leadership evolution?" If you have read this far, you have already started building your personal leadership model. Here are some thoughts on starting your leadership evolution journey:

- **BELIEVE:** The purpose of the introduction is to share the value of having a personal leadership model. My hope is that you are now a believer in its importance.

- **START YOUR JOURNAL:** As I mentioned previously, writing in a journal is a terrific development accelerator. I recommend that your journal be your professional and personal development partner from now on. Writing in your journal should extend well beyond reading *Strategic Pause*. You can start your journal by contemplating some *Thinking Questions*:

THINKING QUESTIONS

▸▸ Why do you want to be a leader?

▸▸ Whom do you consider to be a leader? Why do you consider them to be a leader?

▸▸ Are you building credibility or do you demonstrate behaviors that erode credibility?

▸▸ What principles and methods do you think make up leadership?

▸▸ If you put it on paper, what does your personal leadership model look like?

- **TAKE IT IN:** Your selective listening and cognitive filters are now armed. Your mind should now be attuned to the topic of leadership. If you believe in the importance of having a personal leadership model, you will begin seeing examples of leadership and non-leadership everywhere: in your behavior, in the behavior of others, in the characters and plots of books and movies. Everywhere. It is not just coming at you now; you just did not recognize it before. Take it all in. This book will show you how to take these observations about leadership and make them actionable. You will learn about tuning your mind's filter in "Your Reticular Activating System" in *Strategic Alignment* (Part 3.4.2).

- **READ & INTERNALIZE:** Continue reading the book. Think about the content. Determine if and how it integrates with your personal leadership model. Answer the *Thinking Questions*. As I stated earlier, I wrote this book to be read in any order.

- **TAKE INITIATIVE & BE TRANSPARENT:** Leadership is a process, an evolution, not a destination. You should put your increased focus on leadership into action now. Do not wait until you have a draft of your personal leadership model to start. *The Strategic Pause* (Part 2), where we are going next, specifically focuses on leading in the moment. As you build your leadership model out further, adapt your behavior accordingly and do not be afraid to be transparent with your team and those around you. You will hear much more in *Be Transparent* (Part 3.6.3). You will find that your team has their own views on leadership. You will learn from them.

PART 2

The Strategic Pause

The strategic pause is how you lead in the moment. It is the ESA leadership model's method that enables you to lead in the present. It is the link to and the hub of the rest of the model. This makes it the most important component of ESA and a personal leadership model and why it is the title of this book.

The strategic pause has three levels. Level one is "Situation Management & Composure." Level two is "Leadership Templates & Initiative." Level three is "Align to Core & Objectives." In this part of the book we will walk through levels one and two. Level three will be covered in *Methods* (Part 3.5).

2.1 Your Behavioral Model

The root of the strategic pause is your personal behavioral model. It is how you make decisions and govern your behavior. Whether you realize it or not, you do have a personal behavioral model. The only question is whether it is explicit or implicit.

What is an animal's behavioral model? It is instinct. It is "fight or flight." When something happens, they react. In human terms, fight or flight means your behavior is governed by emotion.

What separates humans from animals is the ability to pause and think. We can use reason to consider alternatives. We can plan for the future instead of just living in the present. When something happens, we can respond rather than react. Having reason versus emotion drive behavior is where the strategic pause starts.

THINKING QUESTIONS

» Is your behavior subject to your emotional whims?

» How often do you find yourself in what feels like "fight or flight" situations?

» What is your personal behavioral model?

» How often do you explicitly pause and think?

2.2 Situation Management

If you do not have a personal leadership model and no explicit personal behavioral model, you are more likely to be reactive. Being reactive means that emotion plays a central role in your behavior. If someone yells at you, you yell back. If you are frustrated, you lash out at others in a manner that is out of proportion to the situation.

The first level of the transactional method of a personal leadership model is putting reason at the wheel and emotion in the back seat. It is called "situation management."

Situation management originated with Benjamin Franklin. Ben was very dynamic; he enjoyed being an expert in many fields. He frequently found himself wanting more time for his various interests, and he contemplated how to get the most out of the time he had.

Ben reasoned that when you break time down, it is composed of a series of situations and events. You have limited control over which situations you are presented with, but you do have control over how you respond to each situation. That response will drive or influence the outcome.

Note that I use the word respond versus react. Reactions are frequently destructive while responses are designed to be productive. If you respond, reason and logic are in control. You think before moving forward. If you react, emotion is in control and driving your behavior. Your day is managing you rather than you managing your day.

Situation management can be simplified to this formula:

$$S + R = O$$
Situation + Response = Outcome

If you are not a big fan of formulas, you can also express situation management as:

Respond, Don't React
Evaluate, Minimize Emotion, and Choose Response

I like "evaluate" and "choose" because they reinforce the central role of pausing and thinking. By thinking through your response to a situation, you are maximizing your control over the outcome. Given that your day is a series of situations, that outcome will often lead directly to the next situation. Thus, situation management maximizes your control over and management of your time.

In my years of leadership coaching, situation management is one of the concepts that resonates most with my mentees.

Situation Management in my Childhood *(Leadership Example)*
I was first exposed to a form of situation management as a child by my dad. Whenever I would go to him with a question or problem, he would rarely give me the solution right away. Instead, he would tell me to "think." My inquires would range from how to draw a perfect circle to why my bike had a flat tire and how to fix it. If Dad thought I did not have enough knowledge or skill to figure it out, he would ask leading questions like, "Did you try to pump up your tire? Try that and see if you can find the leak." I started taking pauses before asking my questions or raising issues. I would first see if I could figure it out.

Dad's approach emphasized systems thinking. In simple terms, when something needs fixing, first you have to figure out how it works by understanding how the different components interact with each other. Systems thinking is an important part of the strategic pause. If we choose a particular response, what are the cascading impacts? What happens next and then after that?

The Unsent Angry Email *(Leadership Example)*

We have all been in this situation. You get an email that upsets you. Someone at work is pointing fingers to deflect blame from themselves. Or, someone made a bad decision that could have been avoided if they had had a simple conversation with you. You would be justified in sending a strong reply pointing out their error. However, that would escalate the situation and be unproductive. You may even write the email blasting them and not send it, just to vent your frustration. After giving yourself time to cool down, however, you write the proper response designed to move the situation in a constructive direction. This is situation management in action.

The truth is that you have been practicing situation management and did not even know it. It is the way most people approach their day-to-day decisions. Few people are completely ruled by their emotions. That said, few have made their behavioral model explicit and, because of that, they are susceptible to being reactive. Since you are now building your personal leadership model, your vulnerability to being reactive is greatly reduced.

Situation Management & Composure

Being cool and composed is the level one strategic pause. When asked what qualities a leader should possess, the majority of people will include "composure." It is one of the most important qualities of leadership. Can you think of someone you consider to be a leader who does not have this quality? People will not follow someone who tends to lose control.

How do you develop the quality of staying composed? How can you maximize the chance that you will be cool under pressure? The answer is situation management: "Stop. Think. Lead." When you lose your cool, you are reacting; your emotions are in control. If you practice situation management, you stop, think, and choose how to respond. You are in control and your behavior is based on reason and not emotion. Your response is how you are leading in that situation.

Even the greatest leaders cannot be cool and composed one hundred percent of the time. When they do lose composure, how do they recover from it? They admit their lapse, assess the damage, and move forward. Sometimes there is a silver lining in that a small, temporary loss of self-control can make them seem more human to their team. You will lose your composure in front of your team at some point. You are not perfect and should not hold yourself to that standard. Practicing situation management will make those occurrences as infrequent as possible.

Staying Composed in a Cube Farm *(Leadership Example)*
I started my career as a mainframe programmer for a pioneering database marketing firm, writing programs that would process millions of records. The biggest jobs would run over the weekend. One of my programs was being run as part of a larger update cycle. I had tested it thoroughly, but I was still nervous because this was a first for me. Throughout the process, I had worked closely with the business systems analyst who had pulled together the functional specification and signed off on the testing.

Monday morning came and I was excited to see what had happened over the weekend. Shortly after I arrived, the analyst showed up at my cube and, in a loud, angry voice, announced that my program had taken down the whole update over the weekend. Heads instantly popped up across the cube farm. My initial reaction was to feel defensive. I had double and triple checked everything.

I suppressed my defensive reaction. Instead, I chose to stay composed and calmly asked what happened. I immediately took the lead in trying to identify the root cause of the problem and started to think about how to recover. The update failed because the analyst failed to properly move my code into production from development. My internal reaction was pushing me to blame him, but that would have been counterproductive. As expected, he backed down when he understood what had really happened and, shortly thereafter, apologized for his reaction. I began to build a reputation for remaining composed. My response to simply lead the remediation of the issue is an example of situation management and composure.

Witnessing my Mom's Composure *(Leadership Example)*

When it seemed like time for my great grandmother to go into a nursing home, my parents decided against it. Since Mom was a registered nurse, she had the skills and experience to provide the needed care. She put her career on hold and Grandma moved into the den off of the kitchen.

It was mid-August, I was eleven, and Mom and I were the only ones home. Mom went to check on Grandma and found she had stopped breathing. Mom called me into the den and issued clear instructions to get the CPR board from behind the bookshelf. I helped roll Grandma onto her side so we could put the CPR board underneath her. I then witnessed my mom perform CPR and bring Grandma back.

This experience had a big impact on me. In particular, I was extremely impressed by Mom's composure in a life-or-death situation. For me, this established a clear connection between composure and leadership.

Raging on the Inside Only

Keeping control, especially when you are new to the concept of situation management, is easier said than done. While you are controlling your behavior on the outside, you may be raging on the inside. Practicing situation management does not mean you will have achieved inner peace. That said, I have found that you get a whole lot more of that as you gain greater control of your emotions and behavior.

Releasing the Positive

Negativity and its associated reactions are destructive. Positivity has the opposite effect. Expressing positive emotions can add energy and even humor to a situation. They are seen as optimism and enthusiasm and, because of this, I usually let positive emotions flow into my behavior. Note that I am responding—not reacting—because I am choosing to allow the positive emotions out. The level one strategic pause (situation management) is the governor that does the quick check of whether emotions are positive or negative. We will cover further in *Be a Positive Force* (Part 3.6.1).

THINKING QUESTIONS

▸ How much do you allow emotion to drive your behavior? Do you react or respond?

▸ How often do you feel the need to apologize for behavior that was emotionally driven?

▸ In moments of truth, are you composed? Do you expend your efforts on taming your emotions or on thinking about how to move forward?

▸ Is there anything stopping you from immediately practicing strategic pauses in your day-to-day?

2.3 Leadership Templates & Initiative

"Leadership Template" is my term for a mental framework or conceptual model. It is a simplification, shortcut, or reminder of a principle or method you may want to use in certain situations. Templates are important tools that enable us to apply captured ideas to broader circumstances. Leadership templates are the first part of the level two strategic pause.

When something goes right or wrong, you need to understand why. Create a conceptual model, a leadership template, for what happened. When something simply catches your interest and you want to better understand it, create a leadership template. Leadership templates can be a few words, some bullet points, or a visual reminder. Quick examples include:

- "On Time": A Post-it Note on the edge of your computer screen as a reminder that you struggle with punctuality.

- S + R = O: Situation management expressed as a formula.

- ESA: The leadership model of *Strategic Pause* is an integration of multiple leadership templates.

The third bullet point needs to be reinforced. Leadership templates are the building blocks of a personal leadership model.

ESA Process

I mentioned in *How do you build a personal leadership model?* (Part 1.7) that ESA has three applications. You already know that "ESA" stands for "explicit, simple, and actionable," which are the qualities of a personal leadership model. Here, we explore the second meaning where ESA signifies a process. It is the process you use to create leadership templates.

You create leadership templates when you want to understand something better and apply that understanding more broadly. When you took notes in school, for example, you rarely wrote down the lecture verbatim. Instead, you captured the key points. You isolated the semantics from the syntax. In fact, "syntax and semantics" is a leadership template.

The ESA Process is:

1. **BE EXPLICIT:** When presented with a new concept that has value, start by taking notes to make it explicit.

2. **SIMPLIFY:** Once the new concept is recorded, you have a rough conceptual model. The next step is to determine if the concept can be expressed in more basic terms. The goal is to express it in the simplest form possible. As referenced in "My Leadership Journey" in *Why should you listen to me?* (Part 1.6), reduce it to first principles.

3. **MAKE IT ACTIONABLE:** Now that the new concept has been simplified in your own words, figure out how it can be made actionable. Are there specific situations where you think it would be useful? Should it be integrated into your personal leadership model?

No Big Thinking Sunday Night & Monday Morning
(Leadership Template)

At one point in my career, Sunday nights and Monday mornings were tough. Because things were stressful at work, I dreaded the transition from the weekend to the work week. I found myself riding a rollercoaster: feeling awful at the beginning of the week and fine by the end. I would go from "How am I going to survive the week?" to "I actually got a good deal done!" This was happening every week and the ups and downs were draining. I knew I needed to make an adjustment.

I started by explicitly acknowledging and articulating the situation: the "be explicit" step of the ESA process. Moving to the "simplify" step, I realized that I was allowing emotion to cloud my perspective early in the week. On Sunday nights and Monday mornings, I was focusing on all the challenges I was going to have to face. I tended to trivialize the positive and give too much influence to the negative during this period. I was allowing my emotions to have free rein. Moving to the "make it actionable" step, I decided to stop thinking about the challenges at those times. The long-term solution was to not allow negative emotion to have as loud a voice. But, while I worked on that, I decided to act by putting this leadership template in place. The impact was dramatic and immediate.

One example was setting growth targets for each of the accounts in my division. I set the targets on Sunday night, allocating only 50 percent of the division's overall growth target. When I returned to the task later in the week, I realized that my negativity caused me to only account for the growth opportunities that had a near 100 percent chance of closing. I would have saved myself time and stress if I had followed the leadership template and set more realistic and positive targets later in the week instead of Sunday night.

Another example was my self-evaluation for an annual review. One year I drafted it early Monday morning. My negativity caused me to trivialize my impact on my team and business. In revisiting it a few days later, I confidently doubled the number of results listed and better explained which of my strengths were on display. Again, I would have saved myself time and stress if I had followed the leadership template and wrote my self-evaluation later in the week when I had a more positive perspective.

Situation Management & Leadership Templates

Leadership templates are put into action by situation management. In situation management, you choose to respond rather than react. By using leadership templates, you add more depth to determining your response. You do not just choose the first one that comes to mind: you consider alternatives first. Leadership templates are helpful in flushing out alternative responses. In fact, after choosing not to react, the next step in situation management is browsing your inventory of leadership templates. You are adding depth to the R of the "S + R = O" formula.

Efficient Errands *(Leadership Example)*

When you run errands, doing a bit of planning can make a big impact. If you need to go to four different places, for example, you do not jump in the car and drive to the first place that comes to mind. Instead, you think about the four different locations and make a plan. You may choose an order than minimizes driving time or you may go to the grocery store last since you will buy items that require refrigeration. There are many possible factors. You will choose the route that takes those factors into account. The point is that you have taken a strategic pause to consider the possibilities.

Can vs. Can't Control *(Leadership Template)*

This leadership template comes directly from my father-in-law, Ron Plante. It is simple and powerful. When confronted with a new situation, determine what you can and can't control. Focus on what you can control. Then, take what you can't control, put it in a can (as in metal storage container), and put it out of your mind (put the can on the shelf). This is easier said than done, but it gets easier with practice.

This leadership template can also be used to determine the difference between pressure and stress. Pressure is good: you increase your focus on what you can control. Stress is thinking and worrying about something that you cannot control. Stress is bad: it steals mental throughput and energy.

Strive to identify the difference between pressure and stress. If you are under pressure and you care about the outcome, do everything you can reasonably do to impact that outcome. If you feel stress, do everything you can to get those thoughts out of your mind. Like I mentioned earlier, this is easier said than done. If you practice using this leadership template in situation management, you will get there.

Know When Good Enough is Good Enough *(Leadership Template)*
It is sometimes difficult to know when to stop working on a task. Should you add more data or formatting to the spreadsheet? Should you reorder the slides or change the colors and theme? When you care about an assignment, you can devote every minute of your time right up until it is due.

Every assignment has a goal and your primary focus should be on achieving that goal. Once you think you have accomplished that, you may decide to add value by doing more. You can anticipate possible questions and include related information. You can tune the format in an attempt to communicate the key points even more clearly. But when do you stop?

Take a strategic pause and apply the "know when good enough is good enough" leadership template. If you believe that you have achieved the goal, consider moving on to other tasks. Ask yourself if dedicating an incremental hour would yield greater value to the current assignment or if it would have greater impact on a new task.

I also refer to this leadership template as "The Curse of trying to be Perfect" or "The Challenge of trying to be Fully Comprehensive." I have repeatedly used it while writing this book. I want the wording to be perfect so, as a result, I have edited certain sections over and over. I finally stop when I ask myself if the content is good enough. Is the primary concept being clearly communicated? If the answer is affirmative, I start focusing my efforts on other content.

Take Initiative & Challenge the BAU

Leveraging leadership templates is the first part of the level two strategic pause. Taking initiative is the second part. So far, the strategic pause has been focused on helping you respond more intelligently to situations as they arise. Taking initiative makes the strategic pause more proactive. Instead of waiting for the opportunity, you seek out situations to add value.

Your greatest opportunity to take initiative is to challenge business as usual (BAU). Instead of taking the well-worn and well-documented path, you should proactively consider alternatives. You may end up on the BAU path, but you will be taking a strategic pause instead of pushing forward automatically. At the very least, you will have validated that the well-worn path is still the best one. But, you may be surprised by how often you find a better one. Leveraging leadership templates and taking initiative to challenge the BAU within your strategic pauses is adding depth to the "Think" and "Lead" parts of "Stop. Think. Lead."

Writing My Leadership Book *(Leadership Example)*

This leadership book is my passion project. It has been my aspiration for more than ten years. Year after year, I made limited progress. I was allowing life to get in the way. So, I took a strategic pause and decided to take a professional pause with the key objective of finishing and publishing my book. Without the increased focus, it would not have happened. My strategic pause made *Strategic Pause* happen.

The Secure Data Hub & PCI Compliance *(Leadership Example)*

One of our large financial services clients required their platform to store credit card numbers. This meant the platform needed to be Payment Card Industry (PCI) compliant.

The BAU approach to attaining PCI compliance was to add layers of security to any part of the system that interacts with or stores credit card numbers. It would have been a massive effort. Instead of forging ahead, we took a strategic pause. The client did not need credit card numbers stored across the system. By better understanding the client's needs, we came up with a better solution. Instead of bringing the entire system up to PCI compliance, we created a new component dedicated to PCI compliance called the "secure data hub." Whenever inbound data contained credit card numbers, we passed it through this secure data hub. Encrypted card numbers were stored on the hub and the rest of the data was passed to the larger platform with card numbers removed. If outbound data required credit card numbers, it passed through the secure data hub to have it appended. Bringing the entire platform up to PCI compliance would have been a nine-month effort. Building the new secure data hub took one month. This novel approach quickly became the standard architecture to achieve PCI compliance for all other platforms.

Effective over Efficient *(Leadership Template)*

Your team is ahead of schedule on a big project, which means you are going to have excess capacity become available. Having your team sit idly by is not an option. If you are a good manager, you have a running list of projects you can attack when you do have excess capacity. How do you decide which project to assign?

Choose effectiveness over efficiency. Effectiveness is doing the right things. It is being focused on the most impactful destination. Efficiency is doing things right. It is being focused on the shortest path to the destination. Effectiveness will have a greater impact on the long-term. If you are headed in the wrong direction, it does not matter if you are efficient. When you are headed in the right direction, you can focus on shortening the trip.

One example would be having your development team focus on adding reporting functionality to your customer interface (effectiveness) versus reducing the update time of the application by twenty percent (efficiency). I am not saying that efficiency is not important. I am saying that when deciding between two seemingly equal alternatives, where one impacts effectiveness and the other impacts efficiency, choose effectiveness. In this example, however, if you are losing customers because your updates are taking too long, you should choose to focus on update efficiency. In that case, the two alternatives would not be equal.

THINKING QUESTIONS

▸ Are there particular pieces of advice you find yourself sharing with others? Is that advice a leadership template?

▸ What leadership templates do you use over and over?

▸ Are your leadership templates in explicit and simple terms?

▸ Where are the gaps in your inventory of leadership templates? In what situations do you struggle to figure out what to do next?

▸ How often do you challenge business as usual? Are there times you see potential improvements but do not speak up?

PART 3

The ESA Leadership Model

In *How do you build a personal leadership model?* (Part 1.7), you were introduced to "Classroom Leadership Evolution" and the five high-level steps of building a personal leadership model. We covered the first two steps, *The Strategic Pause* and *Leadership Templates* in Part 2. In Part 3, we cover the remaining steps. Step three is defining your leadership model framework. Step four is filling in the framework with principles and methods articulated in your own words. Finally, Step five is recognizing that leadership is a process and not a destination. It is evolving your leadership model based on your experience and circumstances and making sure you keep an open mind so that you are continuously learning. Step five is represented by this entire book.

To start, we will discuss how a leadership model evolves and how you measure its evolution.

3.1 Leadership Model Evolution

Your personal leadership model is an integration of multiple leadership templates. How do you evolve those leadership templates that make up your personal leadership model and thus evolve your personal leadership model overall? How do you measure your progress?

Evolution Scenarios

You build and evolve your personal leadership model by assessing it against leadership templates that you come across or create. If you determine that a new leadership template is important, you consider integrating it into your personal leadership model. This integration process has four possible scenarios:

1. **ADD:** You determine that the new leadership template is not accounted for in your leadership model. In this case, you add it to your model.

   Situation management is an example of a leadership template that I added to my leadership model. It evolved into the strategic pause.

2. **MODIFY:** You determine that the new leadership template is partially accounted for in your model. In this case, you add bullets to your existing templates, or you fine tune the language to include what was not covered.

   "Be Cool & Composed" is an example of how I modified ESA. Composure used to be an explicit core value. *Core Values*

(Part 3.3.1) will be discussed in *Foundation* (Part 3.3). Recognizing that situation management is the method behind staying composed, I realized that I had composure listed twice. I decided that composure should be covered by situation management and removed it from core values.

3. **DELETE:** You determine that the new leadership template is already accounted for in your model. This goes back to my comments on management fads in "Transforming Gray into Black and White" in *Introduction* (Part 1). The idea is already there but expressed in different words. In this case, you do not need to change your leadership model. You can disregard the new leadership template.

As I mentioned earlier, most leadership books cover situation management in some form. I have come across other articulations such as "Think before you act" and "Live in your rational mind." Since I already captured the method in language that I prefer, I disregarded these other articulations.

4. **SAVE:** You determine that the new leadership template is not accounted for in your model. You also determine that it is not important enough to warrant adapting your personal leadership model. In this case, you should save the new template for possible future use. Capture it on a secondary list that is not part of your current model.

Over the years, I have saved a great number of leadership templates that are not in ESA. My inventory is over 50 pages. I have grouped them by categories such as strategy, people management, project management, and organization. If I am stuck on how to deal with a situation, I refer to this inventory for leadership templates to provoke thinking. I share a number of these templates throughout this book.

The Skills Pie *(Leadership Template)*

The skills pie is an example of one leadership template that is in my inventory but not explicitly in my leadership model.

Skills come in three types: conceptual, interpersonal, and technical. Conceptual is the ability to think; it includes understanding, simplifying, organizing, and creating. Interpersonal is the ability to relate and communicate. Technical is knowing how to do something specific, such as programming in a specific language or using a spreadsheet application. When comparing skills pies, you can identify opportunities for professional development. In my leadership coaching, I challenge my mentees to create multiple skills pies. Which skills are they using today to add value and at what percentage? What do their current and future roles require in terms of skills pies? Note that pie sizes will vary based on the person's skill set.

Below are three sample skills pies. The assigned percentages are my interpretation.

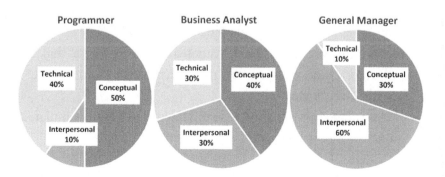

In *Leadership Model Framework* (Part 3.2), we will walk through the framework and add more structure to the ESA leadership model. Through the rest of Part 3, we will fill in the framework with leadership templates. As mentioned in Part 1, you will make it your own. You will decide if you agree with the framework or adjust it accordingly. You will decide if you prefer different principles or methods to populate the framework. Most importantly, you will be building your own personal leadership model.

Evolution via Red, Yellow, Green

As you build your personal leadership model, you will include principles and methods that you have already internalized. You will also include principles and methods that are aspirational: they are important to your model, but you have not yet internalized them. You are not yet behaving in accordance with them.

You should include both the internalized and aspirational principles and methods in your model. But, you should highlight the aspirational components as works in progress so that they stick out as a reminder that you are still internalizing them into your behavior.

While I strongly believe in using quantification to measure progress, doing so can be tricky with conceptual principles and methods. You can waste lots of time trying. Most people striving to lead have a good general sense of how they are doing. By being objective, you can evaluate your progress by assigning a red, yellow, or green grade to each principle and method in your leadership model. You should also ask your team and peers for that red, yellow, or green assessment. In my experience, this grading is usually directionally correct.

I leverage the "Effective over Efficient" leadership template to guide my red, yellow, and green grading:

- **RED:** You are neither effective nor efficient. There is a gap in your leadership model.

As you may recall, when I first started to build a personal leadership model, I thought I was technical and, therefore, not strategic. I knew my leadership model needed to have a strategic component, but I had no idea how to fill it in. As a result, I graded myself as red in that area. My plan to go from red to green was to get an MBA and read everything I could get my hands on about setting objectives and creating strategy. Today, I have definitive perspectives on strategy which I will share in *Strategic Alignment* (Part 3.4.2).

- **YELLOW:** You are effective, but you could be more efficient. You get results, but it takes too much effort for you and your team.

Staying ahead of your daily scramble can be exceedingly difficult because your work queue is typically much larger than your work capacity. I have been in this situation numerous times in my career. I graded my personal productivity as yellow during those times. Personal productivity is making sure you focus on what is truly important and maximize your personal output. When your personal productivity is yellow, you need to revamp your personal organization system. I responded to being yellow by reading *Getting Things Done* by David Allen, a leading expert on personal productivity, and by asking others to share their systems and secrets. I continually tinker with how I organize my to do lists and the processes I use to review and update them. Much more on this topic in *Personal Organization* (Part 3.3.2).

- **GREEN:** You are effective and efficient. You are proficient. You have internalized the principle or method.

The strategic pause grades out as green in my personal leadership model. Given that it is the title of my book, I should hope so!

As you build your personal leadership model comprised of principles and methods, objectively grade out where you are today in relation to where you want to be. If something is red or yellow, this process essentially sets your development objectives for you. When you first start out, you will not be able to focus on all the red and yellow areas at once. Focus on one or two. The "Effectiveness over Efficiency" leadership template will be helpful.

THINKING QUESTIONS

▸ How do you internalize constructive feedback?

▸ Is your personal and professional development plan implicit or explicit? Is it on paper?

▸ What does your skills pie look like? What would you like it to look like in three years?

3.2 Leadership Model Framework

What does a leadership model look like? The starting point is ESA's leadership model framework. The framework gives ESA form. You have already been given multiple hints:

- A leadership model contains *principles* (the objective, the "what").

- A leadership model contains *methods* (the process, the "how").

- A leadership model contains *differentiators* (your leadership style, the "who").

- A leadership model is focused on delivering *sustainable results*. This means leadership enables consistent long-term results.

- A leadership model helps you both handle what is happening in the present and prepare for the future.

- The *strategic pause* is the hub of the entire leadership model. It is leadership in the moment.

ESA's leadership model framework is a 3x3 grid that covers all the bases of leadership. You need to decide what your personal leadership model framework will look like when you make it your own. You can use ESA's grid as your starting point.

The Grid

The rows of ESA's 3x3 grid are:

- **PRINCIPLES:** This is the "what." The first row contains three principles.

- **METHODS:** This is the "how." The "how" makes the "what" happen. The second row contains three methods.

- **DIFFERENTIATORS:** These are the principles and methods that make up your individual leadership style, the "who." They are the subset of your larger set of strengths that apply to leadership. The third row contains three differentiators. (The differentiators stand alone as ESA's columns do not apply.)

The primary principles and methods, the first two rows, are the pillars of the ESA leadership model. The differentiators are the buttresses: they support and magnify the primary principles and methods.

To make leadership real, you need both principles and methods. Too many leadership books focus primarily on one or the other. As a result, they give an unbalanced view.

The columns of ESA's grid are:

- **FOUNDATION (OPERATIONAL):** In the first column of the grid are the principles and methods that are foundational. They should not be taken for granted. They should be accepted without doubt because they underly the other principles, methods, and differentiators. Because they are always present, they are operational.

- **PRESENT (TACTICAL):** The second column contains principles and methods that apply to leadership in the moment, which is leadership in the present. They are tactical because they are focused on the short and medium term, and their form varies depending on the circumstances. Keep in mind that tactics are aligned to long-term objectives, which are covered in the third column. Since leadership requires followers, the principles and methods in this column tend to be applied to the team.

- **FUTURE (STRATEGIC):** The third column contains principles and methods that are long-term focused. They are leadership in the future. This strategic focus is setting objectives and building the system to achieve them by leveraging the operational and tactical principles and methods within the system.

"Operational, Tactical, and Strategic," a leader's three levels of engagement, is a leadership template. If you strive to lead, you will need to engage at the level that is appropriate to the circumstances. "Principles, Methods, and Differentiators" is also a leadership template.

Here is the ESA grid as described:

ESA
"Know how you impact the big picture"

	Foundation (Operational)	Present (Tactical)	Future (Strategic)
Principles			
Methods		**The Strategic Pause** • Be Cool & Composed • Take Initiative & Challenge the BAU • – – – – – – –	
Differentiators			

Since we have covered the first and second levels of the strategic pause, they are included on the grid. There is a third level to come in *Methods* (Part 3.5). Also note ESA's motto (which we covered in *Why do you need a leadership model?* in Part 1.5) at the top of the grid.

Artifacts are powerful reminders. They can be written or visual. This is the ESA artifact. As we fill in the grid, I will provide this visual with the new content added.

Roadmap

Filling in the ESA grid is the roadmap for the rest of Part 3. Each section will cover two to three cells of the grid in the following order:

- *Foundation*
- *Principles*
- *Methods*
- *Differentiators*

When you map these sections into the grid, it looks like this:

ESA

"Know how you impact the big picture"

	Foundation (Operational)	Present (Tactical)	Future (Strategic)
Principles	**Foundation** Core Values	**Principles** Empowerment (E)	Strategic Alignment (SA)
Methods	Personal Organization	**Methods** The Strategic Pause	Strategic Management
Differentiators	**Differentiators** Be a Positive Force	Simplify	Be Transparent

Note that I filled in the names of principles and methods in each cell to give you a teaser of what is to come.

THINKING QUESTIONS

▸ How does the structure of your current leadership model compare to this framework?

▸ How often do you refer to your personal leadership model to help govern your behavior?

▸ Is your model on display in your workspace as a reminder? Does your team know about your model?

▸ What are your initial thoughts on how the content in the cells of this framework should be filled in?

3.3 Foundation

The foundation contains the operational principles and methods of the ESA leadership model. You may be tempted to take them for granted. However, the rest of the leadership model would be far less impactful if they were not in place. The foundation consists of a set of principles in *Core Values* and one method in *Personal Organization*. Do not skip this section. These principles and methods become more important as your responsibility grows.

3.3.1 Core Values

When the topic of core values comes up, many roll their eyes. They think of a poster in the conference room that no one ever looks at. Core values are much more important than that.

Few individuals and organizations have explicit core values that they live by. Emphasis is on the word "explicit." Those that do have them tend to be more successful. Some of the most successful leaders and organizations have books written about them with at least one chapter devoted to core values or strong culture. Further, when leaders and organizations fail, how often is a lack of living by explicit core values cited as the reason? It is nearly always a factor. What about all the leadership gurus? The majority of their books contain at least one chapter on core values and culture. It reminds me of the famous Peter Drucker quote: "Culture eats strategy for breakfast."

How many people in your network have explicitly defined their core values? How many of them are comfortable sharing and promoting them? How are those who do have them perceived? At a minimum, they have a reputation for high integrity and, as I just mentioned, they tend to be more successful professionally. In my experience, they tend to be happier too.

There are clear benefits to living by explicit core values. Why is it, then, that many leaders and organizations do not explicitly define them and ensure that they are reinforced in the culture?

One answer is that the benefits of core values are not immediately apparent. They are indirect; there will be fewer negative moments of truth caused by straying from core values. Examples of negative moments of truth are hostile workplaces, security lapses, and contractual breaches. If you have explicit core values, your organization is less likely to bear the opportunity cost of those negative events.

When you or your organization are confronted with moments such as these, or with any ethical challenge, you will stand strong.

When I talk about core values, I am not talking about the compliance department. Core values go much deeper than the mandatory training and certification many of us endure each year. They are the common behaviors that we expect of each other every day. Core values are the mandatory minimum expectations.

This lead-up to sharing my core values is, I believe, more valuable than my actual core values. In other words, having explicit core values is the most important thing. Defining yours is an example of you making it your own. If you have not yet explicitly defined them, you can refer to my five core values as a starting point. No matter how you define them, there will likely be heavy overlap with ESA's core values.

Mutual Respect

The Golden Rule: Treat others as you would like to be treated. In a disagreement, whether or not you live by this core value becomes clear. If you consistently violate mutual respect, others will avoid you to minimize your negative impact.

Work Ethic

Leave things at least as good as you found them. If it is your task, you should do everything reasonable to get it done efficiently and effectively. If you do not work hard, why should others trust you to help drive their team, business, or cause forward? You will appear to be unreliable and likely to give up when things get tough.

Responsibility

Earn rewards and accept consequences. If you add value and drive positive results, you should share in the upside. If you make bad decisions that take away value, you should have to weather the downside. Do not expect a reward you did not earn and do not whine about penalties for your mistakes. Responsibility is the feedback loop that improves your personal decision-making.

Integrity

Right over wrong regardless. When the pressure is on or when no one is looking, you still adhere to your core values. You are steady and consistent. Can you think of a true leader who has questionable integrity or does not stay cool under pressure? Integrity, like composure, is always a critical quality of leadership.

Credibility

This is your personal currency. Others believe in you because you have earned their trust. You should always be striving to deepen and strengthen your credibility. If you do not have credibility, people will not follow you.

My five core values should surprise no one. They are self-evident truths. My hope is that you see that core values are worthy of much more consideration than the posters hanging in the conference room.

 Consistent Expectation Setting *(Leadership Template)*
Expectation setting is closely related to core values. It is tied to responsibility and credibility. Over the years, I have even debated if expectation setting should be listed explicitly in my leadership model.

If you are responsible for something, your stakeholders need to know the status. They want to know how things are going and they want to know when you will be finished.

Not setting expectations is not an option. We have all experienced someone going "radio silent." When that happens, we always assume the worst. The most basic expectation stakeholders have is knowing that you will provide updates.

It is acceptable to alter expectations. Everyone understands that circumstances can change. As soon as it becomes clear that you will fall short of an expectation, you should reset it. However, do not make this a habit. You will quickly earn a reputation for being unreliable. If you alter expectations on a regular basis, you need to improve your expectation setting process.

Having a feedback loop is critical to improving your expectation setting. If you are changing expectations, what are the reasons? Could you better control or mitigate the causes? Do you need to build in more time for changing circumstances such as unaccounted for requirements or a less reliable team member? If you are exceeding expectations, what are the reasons? Is there an opportunity to set more aggressive expectations in general?

Understand that expectation setting is tied to the perception of value. If you meet expectations, you have done your job. If you exceed expectations, you have added value.

Core Values Integration

Knowing that self-leadership comes before team leadership, you start by isolating your personal core values. Ideally, you should strive to make your personal and team core values the same. As you will see, there will likely be heavy overlap. How do you isolate and live by your core values? How do you take them to the team level? The process is simpler than you think:

1. **EXPLICIT & SIMPLE:** Isolate your core values through introspection. Once you have isolated them, put them into words and share them with your team as a starting point. Be concise when you articulate them. They must be explicit and simple to ensure they will be understood and adopted. Team core values can be built from the bottom up. Delegate the process to your senior leaders or create a cross-level team. If you delegate this step, you should adopt any output core values as your personal core values.

2. **ON MESSAGE:** At least once per year you should walk the team through the core values. When you roll out the annual objectives, see *Strategic Management* (Part 3.5.2), it is the time to reinforce the core values. You also need to make sure they are part of the onboarding process for new team members.

3. **IN THE MOMENT:** Stay consistent to the core values in your day-to-day. Core values is a leadership template that you leverage within your strategic pauses. Being consistent in small moments will make dealing with big moments of truth easier.

4. **FEEDBACK:** Address team members both when core values are ignored and when they are observed. You can decide the best way to provide this feedback. My preference is to privately address those who stray from them and to publicly praise those who stick to them. Always provide feedback as close to the event as possible.

5. **ALIGNED HIRING:** Since core values are the expectations we have for each other, integrate their assessment into the hiring process. There are all sorts of ways to flush out core values. Ask candidates to share their experiences in high pressure situations. In particular, ask for examples where they stood their ground when forces were working against them. Explicitly ask your gut if the candidate has good core values. In my experience, your gut will often be right. We have all come across individuals whose core values are not aligned with ours. Sometimes companies keep these people around because they deliver results. It is only a matter of time, however, before that individual creates problems for the team or for the company.

If you follow this integration process, you will build two-way accountability. Because your core values are so public, your team will expect you to adhere to them at all times. Because you are steadfast, your team will know that their behavior must stay consistent with them as well.

Ignoring My Gut and the Project Manager *(Leadership Example)*
My client was a top five bank. We were landing a lot of new business and the team was stretched thin. We were particularly short of project managers and we needed to hire quickly.

I interviewed a leading candidate with a perfect resumé. He had deep project management expertise and his technical experience aligned with our platform. Within five minutes, though, my gut started nudging me. Something was off. He had checked all the boxes on paper and seemed to say the right things in the interview. Because of what was on paper and our urgent need, I ignored my gut and hired him. By the end of the first month, I knew it was a mistake.

His project fell way behind, and he required a massive management investment during a time when every hour was precious. He particularly enjoyed taking all of his concerns to HR when they should have been shared with his manager first. In particular, he had a different understanding of responsibility and work ethic. The team was working long hours in an effort to make the dates, but he stuck to a strict forty hours per week. His project updates were more focused on why the delays were not his fault and who was to blame rather than ideas of how to get the project moving in the right direction. He was not a good fit for the team and it took three months to manage through the situation. His misalignment with our core values of responsibility and work ethic is what my gut was nudging me about. Had we screened him better, we most likely would not have made this hiring mistake and saved many people lots of time.

How to Be a Good Person *(Leadership Template)*
One of the greatest compliments someone can receive is that they are a good person. We want our team members to be good people. We especially want the same for our kids. With these tools—practicing strategic pauses and governing your behavior by your core values—you will be seen as a good person.

Strategic Pause + Core Values = Good Person

In situation management's "S + R = O", the R (response) is considering your core values before acting and the O (outcome) is being a good person.

THINKING QUESTIONS

▸ Do you explicitly know your core values?

▸ How would your team define your core values and those of your organization?

▸ How are you going to explicitly define your core values? How will your team, and family, be involved?

▸ How will you integrate the core values into your culture?

▸ Do you generally set and meet expectations? Are there expectations you are unknowingly not meeting?

3.3.2 **Personal Organization**

Why is personal organization in a leadership book? In my experience, everyone will struggle with personal organization a few times in their career. If you strive to lead, you will be challenged even more due to the increased level of responsibility. Being organized means you can focus on leading instead of trying to keep up. You likely have not given personal organization much thought in a leadership context. Leaders rarely cite their organizational skills alongside their leadership skills, which is why I have included them in the foundation section. Personal organization is far more important than you think.

Personal Productivity

Personal efficiency and output are what come to mind. If you are not organized, you are neither efficient nor productive. If you are organized, you have an explicit work queue. You know where you will be spending your time and you will be able to maximize that time. The importance of personal organization, however, goes beyond productivity.

Importance, Urgency, & Priority

Your queue often exceeds your capacity. Personal effectiveness depends on focusing on the right things. When you are organized, you can see which tasks are more important than others and you will be able to set priorities. You will be able to tell the difference between importance and urgency. The email at the top of your inbox is not always aligned with your top priorities. Too often, the urgent jumps to the top of the list. Urgency has a louder voice, but when you compare it to everything else, its level of priority is easier to discern. When you are organized, you can prioritize your tasks and see your critical path.

When you are organized and prioritized, you can also see when you should temporarily stray from your critical path. Sometimes, the most important task is more than you are ready to take on at that moment. If that happens, choose a smaller task that will build momentum. In addition, when you are organized and prioritized, you can see overlap across multiple tasks. You will be able to take advantage of "two birds with one stone" situations. Finally, you will better see tasks that do not need to be done at all. If a task has been on your list for a long time or is clearly a "nice to have," you may decide to drop it altogether.

Being organized goes beyond focusing on what is important and setting priorities. It enables you to better leverage your mind.

Build an External Mind

Your mind is an incredible thinking machine. It is terrific at making decisions and being creative. At the same time, it is a terrible storage device.

Your mind's storage management function is poor. It is not like your online calendar that has reminders for your meetings. Instead, your mind keeps reminding you of things at seemingly random times. It does this until an open item is resolved, regardless of when it is due. This means that remembering and reminding are taking a portion of your mind's capacity and that capacity is no longer available for thinking. Because of this, you are not fully present. This is the cost of using your mind as a storage device.

How do you prevent this? The solution is to build a second mind that is designed to be a storage device.

Your personal organization system is your second mind. It is an external mind. It must be built so that your internal mind believes your open items are being taken care of. To achieve this, your personal organization system must have two components: task lists and review routines. Task lists are where you store all your open items. Review routines prioritize those items for resolution at the appropriate time.

When your mind believes that your open items have been captured and will be revisited at the right time, it stops trying to remember them. Capacity opens up and amazing things happen. You will be more present, more decisive, and more creative. This is because more of your internal mind is focused on thinking. This is backed up by science. I encourage you to look it up.

Credit to GTD

I need to give credit where credit is due. The authoritative work on personal organization, as I mentioned previously, is David Allen's *Getting Things Done*. The concept of building an external mind and my knowledge of the science behind it come from Allen's book. Reading and internalizing his work should be a rite of passage within leadership evolution. I strongly recommend it. Even if you choose not to follow his system, you will walk away with many critical insights about personal productivity.

 Personal Organization System Framework *(Leadership Template)*
Your personal organization system should have two core components: task lists and review routines.

Task Lists

Task lists capture your tasks outside of your internal mind. You will find that having one task list is inadequate. Since all the things you are trying to remember are not created equal, you should store them based on relative importance. My personal organization system has five levels:

- **NOW:** These are the tasks I need to do right now. My timeframe is to complete the tasks today, though yours could be different. I strive to have a realistic number of items to accomplish each day. Avoid the temptation of putting too many things on this list. You will have a different perspective when you check everything off your list for the day versus transferring tasks to the next day.

- **NEXT:** These are the tasks that need to be done but not necessarily today. The timeframe for my "Next" task list is to complete the tasks within the next 30 days.

- **LATER:** These are tasks that I want to capture but do not have a specific timeframe for getting them done. Many of these "Later" items could even be put on a "Maybe" list. In my system, I have combined the two lists. They are items I may find useful to tackle in the future.

- **CALENDAR:** My calendar is only for meetings. I do not want to forget to prepare for and attend meetings. Thus, my calendar is an important list of reminders. I do not store tasks on my calendar, though many people do. If you do, your calendar is also a "Now" or "Next" task list.

- **REFERENCE:** This consists of notebooks, folders, pages on OneNote, directories on OneDrive, and folders in my email. These are the least structured of the five lists. I dump information here if I think I may need to look it up in the future. I spend little time organizing it. "Reference" is not technically a task list. It is the filing cabinet of your personal organization system.

Review Routines

Once all your open tasks are captured on lists, your review routines will prioritize and remind you when a task needs your focus. This is where many people falter. A list is useless if it is never looked at. My personal organization system has a review routine associated with each of my task lists:

- **NOW = DAILY:** I create a new "Now" list every day. The frequency works for me, though yours may be different.

- **NEXT = WEEKLY:** I review and update my "Next" list every Monday. Based on that review, I set priorities for the week. It informs my "Now" list.

- **LATER = MONTHLY:** I review and update my "Later" list once a month. I decide which tasks to pull into my "Next" list and delete items that I no longer think are needed.

- **CALENDAR = DAILY & WEEKLY:** I review my calendar every day to know where I need to be and when. I also review and update it every Monday for the next three weeks. I resolve meeting conflicts and remind myself of meetings that require advance preparation.

- **REFERENCE = AD HOC:** I do not have a regular review routine for my reference lists. I refer to them when I am searching for information. Again, I do not give much mindshare to them. The information is there if I need it.

Note that the "Review Routines" frequency is greater than the horizon of the associated "Task List." For example, your "Now" list holds what you want to accomplish today, but you will look at it throughout the day rather than just once. As your days and weeks unfold, you will be adding, updating, and deleting items from your lists all the time. I used to have a printed summary of my task lists for note taking, but my current system is entirely online in OneNote.

Evolve Your Personal Organization System

The purpose of your personal organization system is to enable your internal mind to be a thinking machine. When you sense that your mind is distracted by trying to remember things, it is time to update your personal organization system. If your system consistently falls out of date, it is time for you to tune or revamp it. Ideally, your system will be so integrated into your daily routine that it will stay up to date by default.

Remember that time spent organizing is time not focused on priorities. Operationally, your personal organization system should strive to minimize time actually organizing and maximize time dedicated to adding value. Spending too much time on the administration of your system is another indication that it is time to tune or revamp it.

I have tuned and revamped my system many times. For example, the timeframe of my "Now" task list changes according to my role and responsibilities. Today, it is daily. In the past, it has been a three-day or a weekly timeframe.

 Choose Important over Urgent *(Leadership Template)*
I already covered this concept earlier, but it is worth reinforcing. As leaders, we have broad responsibilities. There are numerous inbound requests for our attention. All requests

are not created equal, however. Some are important; addressing them impacts the team and the business. Some are urgent; they demand immediate attention. However, just because a request is urgent does not mean it is important. If the request is both important and urgent, though, then it is worthy of climbing to the top of your queue. Otherwise, resist addressing urgency immediately. If you do prioritize it high, you are suggesting that louder volume gets more attention.

In my experience, company politics drives many urgent requests. Someone on your team, for example, may have a negative interaction with someone else in the organization. Their turf may have been threatened and mutual respect violated. Most of the time, these cases seem urgent but are not necessarily important enough to drop everything. Instead, your team member may just need to vent and get some advice. Assessing the political nature of a request helps you determine its level of importance.

 Creating a Win-Win by Reframing Priorities *(Leadership Template)*
As a leader, it can be frustrating when someone tries to make their top priority your top priority. If they frame their top priority in terms of your priorities, you will be more inclined to help. In fact, you may see their request as aligned to what is important to you. When you need help, you should take this same approach. If whomever you need help from has the same top priority as you, they will more likely be willing to help. Figure out how to frame your request in their terms. In business speak, you are creating a "win-win."

An example is a client needing some new functionality, like a new report to be added to their dashboard. To meet their demands, you need engineering resources. If you approach engineering with the needs of your client only, you are not creating a win-win. Instead, consider if the new functionality may be desired by the broader client base. Taking this approach articulates a much stronger case that helps the business beyond just your client, and it creates alignment with engineering's priorities.

Another example is when you assign a new and challenging project to your team. If your team only sees the project in terms of the challenging development effort, you are not creating a win-win. Instead, consider providing broader context. The team will more enthusiastically take on the challenge if they understand that the project can open up new growth opportunities for the company or provide learning opportunities that help their personal career growth.

Note that "win-win" is often referred to as "two birds with one stone."

Organized at the Appropriate Level *(Leadership Template)*
Your level of organization should be tailored to the needs of the situation. It is not necessary to be organized to the maximum degree in all areas. How you organize your home is a classic example.

The clothes in your dresser are organized for instant access. You need socks every day so it should take just seconds to grab some. The pots and pans in your kitchen are organized for medium access. You do not use all of them every day or even every week. You should be able to find what you need in a few minutes. The holiday decorations in your attic are organized for periodic access. You use them at different times, but usually once a year. It may take longer to locate and pull out the particular decorations you need. Further, it is OK to have to hunt around in the holiday containers; they do not need to be organized down to exactly which decoration is in which box. When you organize something more than is needed, you are expending effort that could be more productively leveraged elsewhere.

 Beware of False Obligations *(Leadership Template)*
An important part of personal productivity is not doing things unnecessarily. Put another way, do not burden yourself with false obligations. False obligations are things you think you should do but are actually optional. Since you keep them on your mental list, they steal energy from other things more deserving of your focus.

It could be that half-read book that you do not really like but feel obligated to finish. When you see a new book you would like to read, you dismiss it because you think you need to finish the other one. Donate the old book and move on. The same scenario applies to magazines. You have a stack of back issues you plan to review because you worry that they may contain something useful. Some people go halfway by skimming back issues and tearing out items they are interested in. Recycle the magazines. You will be instantly up to date and ready for the latest issue. These ideas also apply to your work. You are probably saving email newsletters of industry trends or the latest blog posts from experts you respect. You feel guilty because you have not kept up. Delete them. By releasing false obligations, you instantly remove the associated guilt.

Be Ready

An important part of leadership is being ready. It means you have a handle on the current state of your team and organization. It means you are rarely surprised by what happens next because you have already considered it. Being ready means you easily fulfill senior management's requests for information (managing up), and your team recovers from challenges and takes advantage of opportunities more quickly. Being ready has two components.

Status

Like your personal organization system, your status is more important than you think. When I say status, I am referring to your status update routine, which includes your status report, status meetings, and the process of bringing the information together. Even if senior management is not asking for a status report, you should be pulling one together. Note that status will also be covered in *Strategic Management* (Part 3.5.2).

If you are asked for information more than once, you should consider adding it to your status. The information can explicitly appear or live within your personal organization system. Anytime this information is requested, you will have it ready.

The visible value of status is that your superiors will receive updates on your team and your organization. These updates will be in your words, which is critical to managing up. If a status report does not exist, the message going northward is not in your control. This is the secondary benefit of your status report.

The primary benefit for you is that your status update routine is your strategic pause to assess the state of your team and organization. It is a built-in routine that forces you to lift your head up and see the big picture. Put another way, your status update routine gets you outside of the daily scramble and forces you to take a more strategic perspective.

Ready for Due Diligence *(Leadership Example)*

My company was bought by a massive global agency. As the leader of one of the largest divisions, I was pulled into due diligence. Because my team was responsible for a large percentage of company revenue, the buyers had a lot of questions about my accounts. Thankfully, I had the answers because I was already tracking the critical information in my status process. The buyers were asking questions focused on opportunity and risk in the accounts. As the division leader, focusing on the health of my accounts was central to my job and I had already isolated the related metrics. Had I not had that information ready, I would have had to make numerous inquiries of my teams with short turnaround time. I saved them some headaches and was able to provide the information quickly.

Run Scenarios

Running scenarios is critical to being ready. On a regular basis, you should run scenarios by yourself and with your team leaders. What if a critical step or component fails? What if you land more business than expected? What if the critical SME (subject matter expert) resigns? The questions go on and on. Running scenarios can make the difference between being slow and failing and quickly adapting and overcoming. The form that these exercises take does not really matter. The fact that they are happening on a regular basis is more important. Running scenarios is a form of systems thinking, which I mentioned briefly in the "Situation Management in my Childhood" leadership example in *Situation Management* (Part 2.1). Instead of focusing just on the immediate interaction, you consider what may happen next and later. Systems thinking is what separates a manager who handles the now from a leader who prepares for what comes next and farther in the future. Like status, you will hear more about this in *Strategic Management* (Part 3.5.2).

 Big Automotive Client and Scalable Growth *(Leadership Example)* My team built the lead management system for a large automotive company with several well-known brands. This system received leads from multiple channels, qualified where the potential buyer was in the buying cycle, assessed their credit, and determined the personalized treatment they would receive. Each brand within the company, however, had a unique system operated by a different marketing company. The scope of the project was to process leads for just one brand.

While we were developing the brand-specific system, we also considered a scenario where we might be asked to take on the lead management of the other brands. We discovered that, while each brand performed their qualification and treatment determination differently, there were similarities in the base logic. We architected our solution to isolate the decision drivers across all brands so that, if we needed to integrate a new brand, we could do it quickly with minimal programming. Within six months, we got our opportunity. The marketing company handling lead management for one of the other brands went bankrupt. We were able to get their lead management up and running in one week and to do it at a much lower cost. Over the next six months, the rest of the brands moved over to our system. This would not have been possible had we not run scenarios as part of designing the initial system.

Audit Ready *(Leadership Example)*

When you build systems that store customer data, your clients need assurance that you will handle their customer data appropriately. Information security and compliance standards and audits are how clients validate that the data is safe. These audits can disrupt daily operations and be contentious to the relationship. Most companies treat these audits as ordeals to live through. They endure the questioning while offering minimal information. With one of our largest banking and credit card clients, we decided to take a different approach.

Instead of being reactive, we took a proactive approach. We strove to anticipate all of the auditors' questions and provide the information in advance. In a way, we took control of the audit process. While it was initially more work because we were providing more information than normal, this method built trust because the auditors came to understand that we had nothing to hide. The audit meetings went from legal-like interrogations to discussions of security best practices. Over time, we learned which information was truly needed and in what form. Instead of scrambling to get ready for the audit, we achieved a state of always being "audit ready." Beyond increased trust with the client, our audit timelines and level of effort were reduced up to 50 percent.

The Power of Little Habits

I am always impressed by the power of little habits. Big things are not accomplished in single efforts. Break your big tasks into smaller parts and focus on making progress. Use your personal organization system to remind you to maintain that progress. In the process, you will build momentum and before you know it, the big thing will be done.

Ten-minute Rule *(Leadership Template)*

You continually put off things you want to get done. The power of little habits puts a reminder on your task list to make progress. Even when you do that, though, you may still put them off. In these situations, I use the ten-minute rule.

You do not want to do something, but you know it needs to be done. Instead of procrastinating, force yourself to work on it for ten minutes. If you are not engaged after ten minutes, stop. At the very least, you made an effort. However, you may find that you will be fully engaged in the task before the ten minutes are up and end up working on it well beyond that time. You may even complete it.

A good use of the ten-minute rule is for filtering and organizing your home. Use the rule to attack a single drawer, shelf, or box. You will quickly build momentum and move on to another drawer, shelf, or box. If you keep leveraging the power of little habits and the ten-minute rule, you will have a filtered and organized home before you know it.

THINKING QUESTIONS

▸ Do you have a personal organization system that acts as an external mind?

▸ How would you explain your organization system to others? Can you draw its structure on paper?

▸ Does your system need to be tuned or revamped because it often falls out of date?

▸ Do you explicitly set aside time to run scenarios for yourself and your team?

▸ Do you procrastinate on big projects because of the overall effort, or do you kick them off by breaking them into smaller pieces?

Artifact: Below is the ESA grid with the foundation/operational principle and method filled in:

ESA
"Know how you impact the big picture"

	Foundation (Operational)	Present (Tactical)	Future (Strategic)
Principles	**Core Values** • Mutual Respect • Work Ethic • Responsibility • Integrity • Credibility		
Methods	**Personal Organization** • Build an External Mind • Be Ready: Status, Run Scenarios • The Power of Little Habits	**The Strategic Pause** • Be Cool & Composed • Take Initiative & Challenge the BAU • – – – – – –	
Differentiators			

3.4 Principles

ESA is the name of my personal leadership model. I mentioned early on that ESA means "Explicit, Simple, and Actionable." These are the key qualities of a personal leadership model (ESA Qualities). "Be Explicit, Simplify, and Make It Actionable" is also the process that one uses to create leadership templates (ESA Process).

We have now arrived at the original and primary meaning of ESA. The other two came later in my model's development. As I mentioned in the introduction, "E" and "SA" stand for the two most important principles in the model: *Empowerment* and *Strategic Alignment*. In my 25 years of studying leadership, no principles have had more impact. Thus, they hold the most prominent position in my model.

3.4.1 Empowerment (E)

Empowerment is the tactical and team-focused principle of ESA. It applies to both the individual and the team. It will be the basis of your approach to people management.

Maximize Strengths, Minimize Weaknesses

To get the most out of an individual or a team, focus on identifying and leveraging core strengths.

When I say core strengths, I am referring to innate qualities and skills. We are all unique individuals with our own innate strengths. We naturally excel at and seek to leverage these assets. The same applies to teams. A team is composed of individuals whose core strengths are the basis for the core strengths of the team.

Think back to the different phases of your life. What was the root of your successes? You will find common themes—core strengths—that stick out. You will see overlap in what drove your success in high school, summer jobs, college, your first job, etc. You achieved success at higher and higher levels of responsibility, and, at each level, you became better at leveraging your core strengths.

People management focuses too often on weaknesses. I am not saying that you should ignore weaknesses. However, you should avoid or compensate for them if they are innate. In other words, there are things that some individuals will not be good at no matter how much training or experience they have. For example, I would not be a good florist. My innate creative abilities are not the same ones that are needed to be a good florist. Trying to train me or give me experience in that area would only be demoralizing. On the contrary, I am very motivated by simplifying things that are complicated. Simplifying is one of my core strengths. I naturally want to isolate the first principles in those sorts of situations.

The key word here is innate. If a weakness is not innate and is holding an individual back, then you should give it your attention. For example, I could have a client relationship manager who is excellent at building one-on-one relationships, identifying the top priorities, and many other things that drive success in the role. However, they could have poor presentation skills. That gap in their skill set can hold them back professionally. Fortunately, although there are innate qualities that may help, presentation skills can be learned. They are skills that I learned. When I started business school, I was in this exact situation. I realized that I needed to develop those skills, so I forced myself to be the presentation lead for every group project. Today, I actually enjoy presenting.

In my career, I have managed multiple instances where an individual is struggling. Most of the time, they are struggling because they are in a role that is not aligned with their core strengths. They may be working in the data management industry running operations, for example, but their dominant innate strength is writing. I had this situation on one of my teams. At best, this individual was adequate at running operations. If they had been focused on a role that relied on the core strength of writing, they would have performed at a much higher level and would have been more professionally satisfied.

Introspection

Introspection is central to empowerment. Most people can answer the standard interview questions: What are your strengths? What are your weaknesses? Few people, however, really know what their strengths and weaknesses are. There is a big difference between being able to verbalize an answer to those questions and modifying behavior to maximize core strengths and minimize core weaknesses.

Being introspective is easier said than done. Like leadership, it is a process and not a destination. It takes time. You do not suddenly arrive at a point where you completely know yourself and can declare your introspection complete. There will be core strengths that you are able to define but, over time, you will tune how you express and apply them. The same applies to core weaknesses.

This may seem repetitive to the above, but the topic of innate versus non-innate is worth reinforcing. It is sometimes tricky to differentiate between the two. If a strength is innate, seek to leverage it as much as possible. My ability to simplify is an example. If a weakness is innate, you seek to compensate for it because you may not be able to improve. Not having the right type of creative ability to be a florist is a good example. If a skill that is a strength or a weakness is non-innate, determine if you need it and work to develop it. Leverage your innate strengths to develop the non-innate skill. Presentation skills are an example. My innate strength of simplification helped in developing my presentation skills because it enabled me to be organized and craft simple messages.

Introspection is about increasing self-knowledge. What are your strengths and weaknesses? What are your qualities and skills? There are lots of tools out there to help you with introspection, including several online questionnaires. Gallup has built an impressive practice around identifying core strengths. Their "CliftonStrengths" assessment[1] is definitely worth a look. Given the number of resources dedicated to the topic, I am not going to provide an alternative. I will say that you should put anything you discover with these tools in your own words. You will get excited about the output from an assessment and declare, "That's me!"

---

[1] Gallup Inc. "CliftonStrengths." 2020, https://www.gallup.com/cliftonstrengths/en/home.aspx.

Make sure you record the core strength in such a way that it is yours. You will be much more likely to remember it and leverage it. This is just another reminder to make it your own.

 Know Your Resets *(Leadership Template)*
An important skill for a leader is learning how to reset yourself. I am not talking about recovering from physical exhaustion. The only reset for that is time and rest. I am talking about recovering from mental exhaustion.

There will be times in your professional and personal life that you will need to keep moving forward. You may only have a day or a few hours to recover. In those situations, when you reach a point of feeling mentally depleted, what do you do? What activities work best to restore your mental state?

Most often the response is to "power through." You take a short break, grab some coffee or a snack, and keep charging ahead. If you are not completely depleted, you can keep going for a short time. However, over time, the quality of your work will begin to suffer. You may even put yourself in a situation of having to redo that work later.

When it is time to mentally reset, which activities should you rely on? You could take a nap, go for a walk, exercise, read a book, seek encouragement from a confidant, etc. I have three primary resets. I write in my journal, go for a hike in the woods, or ride my bike. When I do one or more of these activities, I feel mentally refreshed and ready to return to the challenge. Note that most activities you use to recover from physical exhaustion also benefit your mental state.

Your Point of Diminishing Returns *(Leadership Template)*

Related to knowing your resets is knowing when you reach your point of diminishing returns. This is the point that your work quality or productivity starts to drop. Each additional hour you work yields less and less output. What do you do when you hit this point? How quickly do you realize that you have hit it? Taking a strategic pause and leveraging this leadership template will allow you to check if you have reached your point of diminishing returns.

When you reach this point, your response should not be to press forward. The value of your output going forward will drop. If you care about the output, you will likely have to redo the work. If you have been introspective, you know when you have reached your point of diminishing returns and you know your resets. Leverage them and return to the task when you will be more productive.

Note that this leadership template is related to "knowing when good enough is good enough" which means being *externally* focused on your impact. Knowing your point of diminishing returns means being *internally* focused on the quality of your output.

Debating on Your Home Field *(Leadership Example)*

One particular leader in my division was behaving on terms that were often in conflict with the interests of the overall team, as well as with the leadership model. We would go back and forth on virtually every initiative. This leader loved to debate verbally. If he was losing the argument on rational terms, he would use various tactics to change the topic or cloud the issue. It was becoming increasingly frustrating. I finally recognized that I was allowing the conflict to be decided on his home field. He was extremely comfortable in a verbal debate format and I was not being tough enough in closing out the issue. As a result, once a debate started to escalate, I shifted the exchanges to email where I could keep the back-and-forth focused on the most important headlines. Once the debate was on my home field, I kept the discussion on rational terms. This strategy reduced the amount of effort it took to resolve differences and increased the focus on moving the business forward. Recognize when you are not playing on your home field and decide if you need to shift the venue. Note that this means you have been introspective enough to be able to define what your home field is.

"Do What You Do Best Every Day"

Another way I articulate empowerment is "do what you do best every day." If you maximize strengths and minimize weaknesses, you and your team will be living by this phrase. If your team can say this, they are highly engaged.

Gallup and other highly respected consulting organizations list associate engagement as the key differentiator that separates good teams from great teams. Knowing and leveraging strengths is a key path to higher engagement. Study after study demonstrates that high associate engagement drives growth and profitability. Over the years, Gallup's work has helped me articulate and refine empowerment's position in my personal leadership model.

Doing what you do best every day also means having a positive perspective. Stay focused on what is there (core strengths) versus what is missing (core weaknesses). This is consistent with the differentiator *Be a Positive Force* (Part 3.6.1).

A Programmer Should Program *(Leadership Example)*

My first management role was being promoted to manager of my programming group. As part of my ramp-up, I reviewed the team's performance reviews and discussed the strengths and weaknesses of each team member with the outgoing manager. Having been on the team, I had come to know my peers well (a few of whom I had trained or ramped up). I respected them and felt I already had a good sense of what they did well.

I was surprised to learn that I needed to pay attention to one team member whose performance reviews were dominated by criticism of their verbal communication skills. This team member was viewed as having poor presentation skills, which led originators of programming projects to request others for assignments. The situation did not make sense to me. I deeply respected this individual, who was an excellent programmer and the fastest coder I have ever met. There was too much emphasis on her weakness and not enough emphasis on her clear programming strength and how to leverage it more.

Weak communication skills were clearly holding her back. As communication is not an innate skill and can be improved, we came up with a development plan. However, while communication skills improved, it was clear that she just wanted to program. Becoming a more polished communicator was not a priority. I started to worry that this programmer would take her considerable talents elsewhere. As a result, once the communication skills reached an adequate level, I decided to take a different approach.

My primary tactic was to pair the programmer with systems analysts who did have strong communication skills in order to compensate. My goal was to allow her to focus on what she did best and let the analysts compensate for weak communication skills. In less than three months, the programmer who had been avoided became the one who was most requested.

The Account Manager with Sales Skills *(Leadership Example)*

Several years ago, I took over the VP-level responsibilities for a credit card client that was only utilizing our email delivery services. I started to get to know our account manager, who seemed eager and dedicated. When I attended meetings with both the client and account manager, I observed much more.

The account manager consistently strove to partner with the client to understand their business needs beyond just email delivery. He flushed out additional ways in which we could help them with new services, both in the present and in the future. His sales and client relationship skills were far beyond his role. Over the next few years, I advocated for more responsibility and the associated promotions.

The account manager became the VP over that account, which had extremely high client satisfaction and remained one of the longest tenured email accounts. And, the client happily leveraged multiple services beyond just email delivery. This individual's leadership was the primary reason for the growth. All he needed was to be empowered.

The Accessible Executive *(Leadership Example)*

When I was promoted into management, I was in awe of my company's senior executives. From my perspective, they had broad responsibilities that I could barely fathom. The head of my division was Brad Neuenhaus. I admired his easy leadership style and looked up to him.

Brad was aware that I was new to management and working fervently on my leadership growth. In our interactions, he took a clear interest in me and my pursuit. It progressed to the point that I could just swing by his office and he would wave me in to talk about leadership. He always made time, despite his busy days.

Having this level of access to a senior executive was extremely empowering. When Brad left to be the president of a smaller company in the space, it did not take long for me to join him. When I progressed to the executive level, I strove to grant the same level of access to my team that Brad gave to me.

Scalability through Empowerment *(Leadership Example)*

There are moments of truth where you need your team to step up and work through a difficult situation. When this happens, do you look to those on the team who are just meeting expectations, or do you ask more of those who consistently exceed expectations? The answer is always the latter. Think of sports teams that look to their top players in clutch moments. Those stars are leveraging their core strengths and are more able to create scale. If your people management approach is based on empowerment, your goal is building a team of stars and rising stars.

We were projected to miss a high-profile launch date on an enterprise database build for a new client with high growth potential. The critical path of the project passed through three developers. Some suggested adding additional developers, but when we considered the ramp-up and coordination, it would have extended the critical path even further. Instead, we off-loaded every non-critical development task in their queues to other members of the team. We also did what we could to ensure that the long hours were as pleasant as possible, which included the general manager delivering pizza on the weekend. In the end, we made the launch date because these three stars shifted into hyper-productive mode.

We also got a secondary but equally important benefit. Instead of complaining about taking on the non-critical work, many of our other team members took ownership of the off-loaded tasks as if they were on the critical path. By supporting the stars, they understood that they were indirectly impacting the big picture. They knew it was an opportunity for them to grow. Not far into the project, some rising stars began to stand out and we were able to leverage them for more of the critical path work.

Empowerment Evolution

Empowerment, like leadership, evolves. There are three levels of empowerment evolution:

- **SELF-EMPOWERMENT:** Self-empowerment is leveraging introspection to isolate and understand your personal core strengths and weaknesses. You strive to position yourself to take advantage of the strengths and compensate for the weaknesses.

- **TEAM EMPOWERMENT:** This is the empowerment of each unique member of your team. Every day, you strive to help them with their introspection and to put them in a position to leverage their core strengths and minimize their core weaknesses. As a manager, you accomplish this through coaching, work assignments, and training.

- **TEAM SELF-EMPOWERMENT:** This is the ultimate goal of a people manager. This is the point where every member of your team is practicing self-empowerment. They know how to maximize their core strengths and minimize their core weaknesses. They put themselves in situations where they can do this. You helped them get there by being a self-empowerment role model and practicing team empowerment.

It is important to remember that empowerment applies to teams overall. If you are the team leader, it is your job to match different strengths and weaknesses to the work. Mixing and matching team members can dramatically affect the whole team's strengths and weaknesses. Keep this in mind when hiring new team members and coaching existing ones.

Value Proposition

Explicitly understand your value proposition and that of your team. Your value proposition is what you do best and what likely differentiates you from your peers. It is the primary way you add value. It is what your clients pay for and why your company pays you. If your team understands their value proposition, they should always seek to reinforce it and never allow it to be put at risk.

Your value proposition is your core strengths or the application of your core strengths. It is directly connected to empowerment. For example, your team's core strength may be "unwavering commitment to quality." Applying that core strength creates the value proposition "reliable delivery regardless of the circumstances." It is a subtle difference worth understanding.

There are some leadership roles where the tactical principle is not team focused. Examples include product management or working as a strategic consultant. Even in those circumstances, however, the empowerment concept of maximizing strengths and minimizing weaknesses still applies. Thus, if you are in one of those roles and are building your personal leadership model, you can still use empowerment as your tactical principle. You may also choose to swap it out. However, you will find that focusing on your strengths will still be central to your approach.

Value proposition will be covered more in the *Strategic Management* (Part 3.5.2).

Situational People Management *(Leadership Template)*
One of the first management training classes I attended was "Selecting Leadership Style" by the Leadership Research Institute.[2] It was a repackaging of work by Paul Hersey and Ken Blanchard from the 1970s.[3] It had a big impact on me.

"Selecting Leadership Style" provided a valuable leadership template for personalizing people management style to an individual team member's situation. Style is selected by assessing an individual's skill and level of motivation for accomplishing a given task. People management can be simplified as four different styles, which are represented in four quadrants.

	Low Skill	High Skill
High Motivation	Coach	Delegate
Low Motivation	Direct	Support

- **DELEGATE:** If the individual has both the skill and the motivation to accomplish the task, delegate. They know how to and want to do the job. Get out of the way.

---

[2] Leadership Research Institute (1995). "Selecting Leadership Style." www.LRI.com.

[3] Hersey, P. and Blanchard, K. H. (1977). *Management of Organizational Behavior 3rd Edition– Utilizing Human Resources.* New Jersey/Prentice Hall.

- **DIRECT:** If the individual has neither the skill nor the motivation to accomplish the task, direct. They do not know how to nor do they want to do the job. You must define the start and finish as well as the steps to get there. The individual executes the steps.

- **SUPPORT:** If the individual has the skill but not the motivation, support. They know how to but do not want to do the job. Emphasizing the importance and context of the task can help. Providing incentive for getting the job done or highlighting the consequences of not getting it done are tactics you can utilize. These situations can be tricky. A big part of a manager's job is convincing the team to do what they were hired to do. How you go about that has a big impact on your team's culture.

- **COACH:** If the individual does not have the skill but has the motivation, coach. They do not know how but they want to do the job. You are there to guide them forward. You should define the start and finish, but only tell them the opening step. They should try to figure out the rest of the steps with you available as a sounding board along the way. Individuals in this quadrant will try to convince you that they should be in the delegate quadrant. If you mistakenly delegate when you should coach, you can hurt their long-term engagement. If you are unsure, start coaching and shift to delegation when warranted.

Your goal as a people manager is being able to delegate to your team because they know how to and want to do their jobs. Delegating does not mean you are a hands-off manager, however. The quickest way to have your team fall out of the delegate quadrant is to ignore them. This leadership template helps you choose your behavior when assigning and managing your team's work queues. It is separate from professional development and performance evaluation, which we will discuss when we cover "Meaningful One-on-ones" in *Strategic Management* (Part 3.5.2).

THINKING QUESTIONS

▸ Can you list your core strengths and weaknesses?

▸ What do your friends and peers say are your strengths and weaknesses?

▸ What compliments and constructive feedback have you been given in the last three months? If you have not received feedback, how can you ask for it?

▸ Think about the last few times you had a great day. What were you doing and what core strengths were you leveraging?

3.4.2 **Strategic Alignment (SA)**

Strategy is largely misunderstood. Many people envision a brilliant leader sitting in an office chair, looking out the window and thumbing their chin. They picture the leader whirl around and articulate some brilliant and infinitely motivating vision. Someone like Steve Jobs typically comes to mind. As a result, people assume they cannot be like Steve Jobs and that strategy is beyond them. But, that leader is a futurist and not a strategist. They are focused on envisioning and articulating the future, which takes specific and possibly innate analytical and creative skills. Thankfully, you do not have to be a futurist to be strategic. I call this misunderstanding the "faux futurist."

Strategy is straightforward. It is setting long-term objectives, creating the plan to achieve them, and rallying the team. Your strategic objectives are typically set one year out.

Many also misunderstand vision. Vision is the same as strategy but set farther in the future. Your vision, your longer-term objectives, should be set for three or more years out. Some may argue that vision is more than longer-term objectives, but I prefer to keep vision explicit, simple, and actionable.

Strategic objectives are milestones in the journey toward the vision.

Sustainable Competitive Advantage

How did I come to this understanding of strategy?

In business school, we studied Michael Porter's "sustainable competitive advantage." It comes from his book *Competitive Advantage: Creating and Sustaining Superior Performance*[4] which

---

[4] Porter, Michael E. *Competitive Advantage: Creating and Sustaining Superior Performance.* New York: The Free Press, 1998.

had a big impact on me. It helped me gain a better understanding of strategy in general. If you are not familiar with the work, I would strongly recommend taking a closer look.

Porter's simplified argument is that an organization's competitive advantage is not sustainable if it is based on leading the market with products or services. If you are the market leader, the competition comes after you. They can examine your offerings to figure out why you are differentiated and successful. They will copy or counter your products or services. You have no choice but to innovate to remain a market leader. And, there is no guarantee that your investments in innovation will be able to keep you ahead of the competition. You are engaged in a ruthless race.

Some companies have been successful at staying ahead by continuing to innovate. Apple immediately comes to mind. It is important to note, however, that android smartphones have taken massive opportunity away from Apple.

Companies that rely on innovation can only stay ahead for so long. Changes in leadership can have a huge impact and economic downturns can cut R&D budgets, which directly impacts innovation. It does not take long to go from leading the market to just trying to adapt and survive. Business history is littered with examples of companies that burst onto the scene with innovative products or services, just to disappear less than ten years later. BlackBerry, Blockbuster, Borders Books, Myspace, Sun, and Netscape come to mind.

There are also a number of companies that have stayed ahead over a long period without relying on innovation. Walmart and Southwest Airlines are two of the most studied examples. What have they done to be successful for so long? The answer is "everything." They have a business model equivalent to what Porter goes on to talk about.

Both Walmart and Southwest understand their value proposition. For Walmart, it is their relentless focus on driving down prices. For Southwest, it is keeping their airfare lower than their competition. How do both of these giants accomplish this? If you look deeply into their organizations, no one thing seems to be the driver. Instead, everything they do drives their success. Walmart puts heavy pressure on their suppliers. The suppliers know that there will always be others who will agree to Walmart's lower cost terms in exchange for having their products in the stores. In this way, Walmart encourages competition. In another example, at Walmart's headquarters, every conference room is painted white and there are often folding chairs because both are the lowest cost options. Southwest flies very few types of aircraft so that they can gain economies of scale in maintenance, and many of their hubs are secondary airports with lower gate-rental rates. If you want to compete with Walmart or Southwest, it takes the total commitment of your organization to the value proposition from top to bottom.

Porter outlines five different forces to consider when striving to build a sustainable advantage. I have simplified his model, his leadership template, as articulating your differentiated value proposition, setting objectives, and cascading those objectives deep into your organization. By doing this, you are building a system. Your value proposition and objectives can be seen at every level of your organization. Everyone in the organization knows how they impact the value proposition and objectives and can better align their behavior.

Breaking into Identification Services *(Leadership Example)*
In the 2000s, my company broke into the identification space. In marketing technology, identification is the ability to connect data sources to create a more complete picture

of the individual. Examples of data sources are a company's customer data (product/services ownership and usage), marketing data (email, direct mail, telemarketing, online, etc.), and credit bureau data. For nearly a decade, our competition had dominated this space. Once we recognized the opportunity, we realized that building an enterprise identification solution was closely aligned to our value proposition. There was complete overlap between building this new offering and building enterprise databases, which we had been pioneering for decades. We went further by enabling greater client customization of the matching logic. The legacy market leader treated the matching logic as secret. It was a "black box." Within a few years, my company was considered a co-leader in the space. Our competitor's offering was not a sustainable competitive advantage.

Your Reticular Activating System

For years, I drove strategy by setting objectives and cascading them into the team. Per ESA's motto, I wanted every member of the team to understand how they impact the big picture. I wanted individuals to see how their own objectives were aligned to the team objectives and how the team objectives were aligned to the account objectives. This "line of sight" went all the way to the overall company objectives.

Cascading objectives is not easy. I was never fully satisfied with our cascade efforts. Too often, they turned into unwieldy administrative exercises that would seem like bureaucracy and compliance instead of creating a clear line of sight for our team members. Yet, year after year, we achieved our highest-level objectives. It did not make sense to me until I finally stumbled upon the reason. It has to do with how our brains are constructed. This deeper level of understanding reinforced that our cascade efforts were not excess administration. They were working well.

Your brain has something called a reticular activating system. It is its executive assistant. It is constantly being bombarded with data from your senses, thoughts, etc. Your reticular activating system is the filter that decides what gets through. For example, if you are sleeping and classical music starts playing in the other room, your reticular activating system lets you sleep. If a baby cries in the other room, your reticular activating system wakes you up because it recognizes that something may be wrong. Your reticular activating system decides what is important enough to get your focus. It is your brain's "focus filter."

You may not know it, but you build your own focus filter. For example, if you love sneakers, you will notice the shoes of everyone who walks into the room, whether you intend to or not. If you like the color green, you will notice anything green in your environment. When you learn an interesting new word, like *empowerment*, you see that word everywhere because your focus filter is now tuned to look for that word.

Set Vivid Vision & Objectives
When you set objectives, you are arming your reticular activating system. You are tuning your focus filter. The second you understand the objectives and how you can impact them, you will be consciously and subconsciously on the lookout for things that are aligned to those objectives. Even if it is a high-level objective, you will automatically strive to put it in terms you can influence.

Going further, your brain is particularly good at repeating tasks. When you set vivid objectives, you trick your brain into thinking you are in familiar territory. The key word here is vivid.

Vivid objectives paint a clear mental picture. When your brain processes vivid objectives, because it can see the picture so clearly, it reverts to "been there, done that" mode.

Vivid objectives have another benefit. They get your brain working for you instead of against you in terms of doing new things. Your brain is always on the lookout for danger. Since unknown situations may contain danger, your brain holds you back. It looks for excuses to not take risks. Vivid objectives paint familiar pictures and allow your brain to accept unknown situations. There are all sorts of studies that prove this. I would encourage you to explore for yourself.

Strategy starts with setting both the vision and the objectives. When you cascade them into the team, you dramatically increase the probability that you will accomplish them. Arm your team's reticular activating systems. Make the vision and objectives as vivid as possible by painting a clear picture and making them quantifiable. Just setting them will make a big difference and you will notice the positive impact.

 The Power of YouTube *(Leadership Example)*
You have been there. You have to accomplish some new task and do not know where to begin. You start by googling the task, and then you remember YouTube. After watching a few quick videos, you can visualize how to move forward.

I could not get the rear derailleur on one of my mountain bikes to shift properly. I tried for two months. I have been adjusting rear derailleurs for decades, but this one was eluding me. I started to wonder if this particular make of derailleur needed to be adjusted differently. To me, they all basically work the same. I watched a three-minute

YouTube video, and my derailleur was adjusted correctly within five minutes. By seeing how it should be done, I instantly saw what I was doing wrong and was able to correct it immediately.

Another example is when I wanted to help my in-laws with their pool maintenance. My family had never owned a pool. But, after watching fifteen minutes of YouTube videos, I had a solid understanding of how pools work, as well as how to perform the backwash process to clean out the filter, which I have performed multiple times since. Again, the vivid visuals allowed my brain to revert to "been there, done that" mode.

 Vivid Vision and Objectives *(Leadership Example)*
There is no one right methodology for developing and setting objectives. I encourage you to explore many approaches. The commonality across all approaches, however, is making your objectives quantifiable. Here are five examples of vivid objectives:

- Close Blue Sky ($15MM) in the Current Year – "Blue Sky" is a business term for revenue growth
- Create 10 Financial Services Points of View by End-of-Year
- Reduce Run Time of the Lead Qualification Module by 33% by Q3
- Conduct a Cost of Goods Sold (COGS) Audit on 15 Accounts in the Current year
- Earn a Green Scorecard in 3 of 4 Quarters

100% Client Advocacy *(Leadership Example)*
In the early 2000s, MIT's Sloan School of Management published articles on customer advocacy. The headline was that customer advocacy is more indicative of business success than any other metric. Customer advocacy is determined by the simple question, "Would you recommend the products or services to a friend?"

Brad Neuenhaus, the president of our company, recognized the power and simplicity of this insight and aligned our entire database services company behind it. His vision was "100% Client Advocacy." He made sure that the whole company understood the objective and how each of us impacts the objective, and he filled our environment with artifacts depicting "100%." He hung various renderings of 100% on the walls and added "100%" tags to the lanyards we used for our company IDs. The reminder was all around us and became part of our culture.

The next year, our small company was identified as a leader in a respected third party's evaluation of marketing database providers, along with much larger companies. We had broken through and our company grew rapidly as a result. Brad's "100% Client Advocacy" vision was a critical driver of the success.

 Best Practices + 1 *(Leadership Template)*
The "follower" strategy is one of the most common strategies. I alluded to it when we covered sustainable competitive advantage. It means not having a strategy of your own, but

instead, surveying the market leaders and copying their approach. This is sometimes modified as a "fast follower" strategy, where the focus is on copying the leader more quickly than other companies.

A better approach than "fast follower" is to enhance the follower strategy as "Best Practices + 1." Take the market-leading strategy and add at least one improvement. Ideally, the improvement originates from your value proposition. You see this strategy across most industries. The proliferation of features in mobile phones and cars are just two examples. When you are setting the objectives and strategy for your organization and team, seeing if you can improve on what the market leaders are doing is a worthwhile exercise.

Cascade Vision & Objectives

When you cascade your vision and objectives into your organization, you are building a pyramid. The highest-level objectives are at the top and the lowest-level objectives are at the bottom. If each level fulfills its objectives, they will cumulatively achieve the objectives of the top level.

Drilling growth objectives into an organization is a good example of cascading objectives. A division with 10 accounts has an annual growth target of $10 million. If each account has equal growth potential, they each have a $1MM growth target. Realistically, the growth potential will vary depending on the size of the account, whether you are considered a strategic partner or an operational vendor, and other factors. One account may justify a growth target of $3MM while another might be $100K. All the account growth targets together will equal or exceed $10MM. Setting growth targets, however, can be trickier than just dividing up the bigger objective. Some accounts will miss their targets while others will exceed their targets. Strive to set targets that take this variability into consideration.

Continuing the growth objectives example: as you cascade deeper into the organization, the objectives will look different. A product manager's objective may be to add functionality to the offering to make it more attractive to buyers and easier to sell. An analytics consultant's objective may be to generate client-specific insights that enable the account and sales leaders to generate interest and escalate within the client organization. The ultimate purpose is for every individual to have objectives that give them a clear line of sight to how they impact the bigger objectives.

Cascading objectives is a task for the entire team. The highest-level leader sets the objectives for the organization. Then each level, with coaching from the level above, sets their own objectives. This should continue until you get down to the individual contributor levels. In the spirit of making it your own, a team member will be more invested in achieving their objectives if they are the ones who set them.

 Cascade as Lead Measures *(Leadership Template)*
Lag measures are the outcomes; they are the results. Lead measures are the inputs; they come first and drive the outcomes. Weight loss is an example of a lag measure. Behaviors, such as diet and exercise, are lead measures that impact weight loss.

When cascading objectives into your team, strive to set lead measures (behaviors) as objectives. Your team will more easily see how they can modify their behavior to impact the higher-level objectives. Building on the growth objectives example from earlier, instead of focusing on the growth number, sales executives could set their objective as calling into clients to make new contacts ten times each week. Product managers could commit to doing surveys of the market-leading functionality once a quarter to see if there is anything to be copied and improved upon.

A Note on Purpose

As you think about empowerment and strategic alignment, your train of thought will take you to the topic of purpose. Purpose is an important part of a personal leadership model. There are numerous books and an entire industry focused on helping you find your purpose. Figuring out what it is and how to pursue it is something you should work on. However, this is a broad and personal topic and not something that one can easily put into explicit, simple, and actionable terms. As a result, I am not going to delve deeply into the topic. As I mentioned, there are abundant resources to aid you on that journey. That said, here are some quick thoughts.

It can take a long time for you to identify your purpose. Your journey has a logical starting point that is aligned with ESA. That starting point is empowerment. If you flush out your core strengths, which is your personal value proposition, and consistently strive to leverage them, you will be on the right track. If, when all is said and done, you can say, "I learned, developed, and leveraged my natural talents (core strengths)," you will have fulfilled your potential and likely have found your purpose. More simply, if you become self-empowered, you are on the path to your purpose.

THINKING QUESTIONS

▸ Do you have objectives for this year? Are they general or vivid?

▸ Do you have objectives for five or ten years out?

▸ Are you reluctant to set objectives because you are afraid you will not be able to achieve them?

▸ What are the metrics driving your organization? Have they been translated into lead measures and cascaded into your team's objectives?

▸ Do you share your objectives with your team and those close to you to increase accountability?

Artifact: Below is the ESA grid with the principles of *Empowerment* and *Strategic Alignment* added:

ESA
"Know how you impact the big picture"

Principles	Foundation (Operational)	Present (Tactical)	Future (Strategic)
	Core Values • Mutual Respect • Work Ethic • Responsibility • Integrity • Credibility	**Empowerment (E)** • Max Strengths, Min Weaknesses • "Do what you do best every day"	**Strategic Alignment (SA)** • Set Vivid Vision & Objectives • Cascade Vision & Objectives – Create a "line of sight"
Methods	**Personal Organization** • Build an External Mind • Be Ready: Status, Run Scenarios • The Power of Little Habits	**The Strategic Pause** • Be Cool & Composed • Take Initiative & Challenge the BAU • – – – – – –	
Differentiators			

3.5 Methods

In Part 3.4 we covered the Principles or the "what" of the ESA leadership model. In this part, we go deeper into the *Strategic Pause* and cover *Strategic Management*, which are the methods or the "how" of leadership. The methods are the mechanisms that enable you to make the principles real.

Taking strategic pauses is leadership in the present. It is leading in the moment. It is the tactical/transactional method of the leadership model. Will you be composed, or will you let your emotions drive your behavior? Will you see a challenge as an opportunity or as a marker of failure?

Practicing strategic management is leadership focused on the future. It is the future/strategic method of the leadership model. It is building a system that creates future moments that will impact the big picture. You prepare for those moments in the present and you exercise strategic pauses when they arise.

Practicing strategic management decreases the occurrence of negative moments and increases the number of positive ones. Negative moments include client-facing issues, attrition of a star performer, or losing business to the competition. Examples of positive moments include advocacy-level client satisfaction, high team engagement and promotion rates, and being awarded business outside of a competitive bid process. By building a strategic management system, you and your team will anticipate and address situations that could become negative moments. You will also recognize and be able to take advantage of situations to increase the value added that might otherwise have been missed. By minimizing negative moments and maximizing positive moments, strategic management drives sustainable results.

3.5.1 **The Strategic Pause**

In Part 2 we covered the first two levels of the strategic pause. In this part, we will cover the final level. It maximizes the "Think" and "Lead" parts of "Stop. Think. Lead."

The strategic pause is the present/tactical method of ESA. You will recall that the first two levels of the strategic pause are:

- **SITUATION MANAGEMENT & COMPOSURE:** Choosing your response and minimizing the influence of emotion. The situation management formula is S + R = O (Situation + Response = Outcome). Responding versus reacting will enable you to remain cool and composed.

- **LEADERSHIP TEMPLATES & INITIATIVE:** Leveraging leadership templates to consider alternative responses. The templates add depth to your decision-making. You no longer wait for opportunities; you take initiative and challenge business as usual.

The third level of the strategic pause is leveraging *empowerment* and *strategic alignment* as leadership templates. It is integrating your core strengths and your objectives into your strategic pauses.

Align to Core & Objectives

When taking a strategic pause and flushing out alternative responses to situations, check the overlap with both your core strengths and weaknesses and with your objectives. Some alternatives will make greater use of your strengths while some will have greater impact on your objectives. Choose the alternative that has the greatest alignment with both.

Think of this level of the strategic pause as performing a quick cost-benefit analysis. Each option has a different level of overlap with your core strengths and objectives and different probabilities of success. Each alternative also has its own level of risk and reward. Avoid any alternatives with high risk and low reward and even those with low risk and low reward. Ideally, you would like to find the low risk and high reward alternative, although there will be times when you may choose one that is high risk and high reward. Consider a new business pursuit as an example. If the prospect is satisfied with a long-tenured incumbent, it is worth taking risks in the pursuit. If you do not differentiate yourself in your pitch, you will lose the business. On the other hand, if you are the incumbent and the client is highly satisfied, it is likely not worth taking big risks that could end up obscuring your established value proposition and threatening your strong position. There is a balance. The point is that when evaluating alternatives, a quick cost-benefit analysis will better inform your decision.

As a people manager, you take strategic pauses on two levels. You make decisions for your team by considering their core strengths and objectives. You also make decisions for yourself by considering your personal core strengths and objectives. Those strengths and objectives may not be the same for you and your team. Make sure you explicitly know the level on which you are applying the strategic pause.

 Leverage Minds and Hands *(Leadership Template)*
To illustrate the highest level of the strategic pause, think of each member of your team in terms of minds and hands. As their manager, are you leveraging both?

The task is to get from point A to point B. As a subject matter expert, you would know the typical steps are 1, 2,

3, 4, 5. As a manager, though, do you assign the task as getting from A to B using steps 1 through 5? If you do, you are only using your team's hands. You are asking them to execute and not to think.

A better approach is to assign the task of getting from A to B and suggest step 1 as a starting point. Your team's job is to figure out steps 2 through 5. Leadership is remembering that they are in their roles because they have the right core strengths and skills to perform at a high level. In this case, you are striving to use both their minds and hands.

You can go further. Maybe your group has the team-level objective of, for example, improving processes by reducing cycle times. If your culture reinforces empowerment and strategic alignment, your team may develop a process that gets from A to B using only steps 1, 3, and 5, reducing the cycle time from five steps to three. Your team innovated because they were free to use their minds and they understood the larger objective.

The highest level of leveraging minds and hands is to assign the task as "A to B" where "B" is a question. In this case, you explain why you believe "B" is the current destination, but you have reinforced a culture that allows your team to question that objective. I have encountered a number of situations where the team suggested a different destination, one that was better aligned to the big picture.

This approach goes back to well-known business writer Ken Blanchard's saying, "None of us is as smart as all of us." If you only leverage their hands, the team is only as smart as you are. If you leverage both minds and hands, the whole team has the potential to be much smarter.

The Efficiency Lunch *(Leadership Example)*

Back to the lead management system my team built for the automotive company (See "Big Automotive Client and Scalable Growth" leadership example in "Be Ready" in *Personal Organization* in Part 3.3.2). Our system received, qualified, determined the treatment, and routed inbound potential buyers. The production cycle ran on Mondays, Wednesdays, and Fridays. It ran for 12.5 hours and sometimes finished the next day. Because the client wanted to follow up with potential buyers more quickly, there were rumblings of shifting to a daily production cycle that would also include Saturdays.

A 12.5-hour production cycle would not allow us to fill this need. Our team objective—speed—became clear, and every member of the team understood the challenge. To provide incentive, I created the "Efficiency Lunch." If any member of the team reduced the execution time of any step in the production cycle by one third, they earned a free lunch for the entire team to honor their accomplishment.

All seven members of the team earned multiple efficiency lunches for the entire team. My lead programmer re-engineered the primary load program three times. In the span of two months, we dropped the product cycle time by 65 percent, from 12.5 to 4.5 hours. When the time came to shift to daily production, we were prepared. The team was empowered and aligned with a clear objective. They had practiced strategic pauses and challenged business as usual. While this is a good example of meaningful recognition, the primary lesson is the power of staying on message with being aligned to core strengths and the bigger objective.

 Lead Them to Their Own Conclusion *(Leadership Template)*
This leadership template is a subset of "Leveraging Minds and Hands" that is worth reinforcing. As a manager, you are often confident that you know the proper next steps for a situation. Resist the urge to direct and allow your teams to do their jobs.

Even when they arrive at the solution you already had in mind, there are benefits. They will see it as their solution and not yours. Their level of ownership and satisfaction from figuring it out themselves will be much higher, and overall team engagement will increase.

Because you allowed them to do their jobs, they also took strategic pauses. There will be times when they come up with a better solution. If you had directed them, you would have closed the door to that innovation. Further, the more you empower and align them, the higher the percentage of time your team will be innovative, reflecting the integration of strategic pauses into the team culture.

Direct your team only when necessary. Use their minds and hands to both empower and strategically align them.

Start by leading them to their own conclusions. You will be pleasantly surprised by the results.

 Balance Process and Results *(Leadership Template)*
Most approaches to delivering a product or service have a bias toward either process or results. As you adjust, you are often aligning your current approach to one more than the other. Ideally, you should be striving to balance the two.

The process is your plan and the results are your destination. If you focus too much on the route, you can lose sight of the destination. Leaning too far toward the process creates administration and bureaucracy. In addition, if you strive to define all of your business processes like an operating manual, your team will be far less likely to innovate because they are just following directions and not paying attention to the objectives. If you focus too much on the destination, however, you can slip into "the ends justify the means" territory. You can burn the team out or build something that is difficult to maintain or repeat. Your new product will be difficult to support if your engineering team quits because you demand all their weekends.

It takes time and tuning to find the right balance between process and results. Your approach will rarely be perfect. It is like a pendulum; it will alternatively favor one side or the other. The objective is to minimize the amount of the swing. Keep asking the balance question. Keep making adjustments. Keep learning.

Strategic Procrastination *(Leadership Template)*

It has happened to you multiple times. You are working on an important challenge or opportunity. The right path forward comes to you while you are taking a shower or walking the dog. Even though you were not consciously thinking about it, you came up with the answer.

This happens when you arm your mind with the details of a challenge or opportunity and then give yourself time. Your focus filter scans your environment for ideas and your mind looks for patterns that connect to other situations and solutions. Usually, this is done accidentally. You are unable to find the answer in one sitting and decide to come back to it later. Why not do it on purpose? When you add a pause in your solutioning process, you ultimately generate more innovative and creative alternatives.

When you apply the third level of the strategic pause to strategic procrastination, you consider your core strengths and objectives when arming your mind.

When Martin Luther King Jr. was writing his "I Have a Dream" speech, he understood this concept. Weeks in advance, he laid out the key objectives of the movement and reviewed historical addresses to arm his mind. He intentionally left writing most of his speech until the night before. In fact, he struggled with and did not author the famous climax until the next day when he sought real-time inspiration from those attending this historic event. Had King written the entire speech weeks before and stuck to the script, it would have been less inspired by real-time feedback and may not have had the same legendary impact.

When confronting a challenge or figuring out how to take advantage of an opportunity, leverage strategic procrastination. Arm your mind with the key information about the situation, consider how your core strengths may be leveraged and how the situation is aligned to your objectives, and then take a break. When you come back to it later, you will have better answers. You may find that you discovered the answer in the shower that morning.

The Strategic Pause and War *(Leadership Example)*
Many years ago, I was reading a book on military strategy and tactics in the early twentieth century. It was the first time I heard the phase "strategic pause." It obviously made an impression on me.

When two armies clash, inevitably one army starts to overwhelm the other. When this happens, the army that is losing will withdraw to limit losses. The business-as-usual reaction of the army that is winning is to pursue and either try to destroy or force a surrender of the withdrawing army.

Instead of immediately pursuing, the army with the advantage should take a level three strategic pause. It is the ideal time to assess the state of its troops (an army's core strength) and to revisit the war and battle objectives. The level three strategic pause is focused on the alignment of core strengths and objectives.

Immediately pursuing the seemingly retreating army could be a mistake. If the objective of the winning army is to hold a beachhead, the losing army could be faking their retreat in order to distract them from their primary objective. Another possibility is that the losing army's withdrawal is designed to change the circumstances to their advantage. In World War II, for example, Rommel's strategic withdrawals in North Africa drew Montgomery into circumstances where Rommel could counterattack with limited risk to his forces. Montgomery thought he was pressing his advantage into Rommel's retreat. Instead, he marched his army into traps.

Even when the next step looks obvious, practice strategic pauses. You may find that your obvious next step may be a mistake and that you should consider alternatives.

"Know how you impact the big picture."

When you build a culture based on empowerment, strategic alignment, and strategic pauses, you are fulfilling the motto of the ESA leadership model.

Your team knows their core strengths and weaknesses. They understand big picture objectives and have a clear "line of sight" through their individual objectives to have an impact. Your team has the freedom, as long as they do not place quality at risk, to take initiative and challenge business as usual. When they choose new paths, they will be aligned with their core strengths and objectives and they will know how they impact the big picture.

Imagine that just one quarter of your team takes this approach. If they each move the team forward an inch, before long the big picture will be impacted. Over time, more and more of your team will take initiative. They will see their teammates taking strategic pauses and making an impact, and they will be inspired to do the same.

A Note on Creativity and Innovation

Creativity and innovation are logical topics in the discussion of having an impact. Similar to introspection and purpose, there are numerous books and entire industries focused on these topics. As a result, I am not going to go too deeply into creativity and innovation.

That said, I do believe that empowerment, strategic alignment, and the strategic pause are the foundations of creativity and innovation. If each member of your team understands their strengths and weaknesses, understands how they are aligned to the big objectives, and has the freedom to practice strategic pauses, you will have created a culture where creativity and innovation are encouraged.

THINKING QUESTIONS

▶▶ Do you consider core strengths and weaknesses when choosing what to do next?

▶▶ Do you understand the big picture objectives of your organization? Are your team and individual objectives aligned to that big picture?

▶▶ How many times a day do you take strategic pauses? Are there opportunities to take more?

▶▶ Does your company and team culture encourage you to challenge business as usual?

3.5.2 Strategic Management

Strategic management is the future/strategic method of the ESA leadership model. It is building a system that creates moments in the future that impact the big picture by leveraging core strengths and creating alignment to objectives. It is composed of nineteen routines that those who strive to lead should be practicing. Think of these routines as your leadership checklist. Examples include meaningful one-on-ones, all-hands meetings, and evaluating/grading out the team objectives.

Before going into the specific routines, we need to cover the structure of the system you are building.

Build a Distributed System

If you strive to lead, you should be building a management system. It is the explicit and simple manifestation of your leadership model. Without a system, you are practicing strategic pauses and leading in the moment. Your team clearly sees that you are leading, but you are largely at the whim of the situations that enter your realm. With a system, you are creating and controlling situations/moments that will enter your queue in the future. Your team sees the structure you are building and how it keeps them more empowered and aligned. Strategic management is how you make your leadership model visible to your team, your clients, and everyone who is watching.

How explicit, simple, and actionable is your system? Have you made sure you are doing everything you should be doing? Do you rely on external reminders, like annual performance review deadlines from HR, to dictate all or parts of your system? If you strive to lead, you should have a management system that puts your personal leadership model into action by making it tangible.

Distributed over Centralized

What form does your management system take? Does the majority of your decision-making take place in a centralized or a distributed system?

In a centralized system, a central team or individual evaluates information, makes decisions, and then hands them down. Remember the leadership example of leveraging minds and hands. Think about a manager who directs and uses only the hands of the team.

A distributed system is the better option. You should be driving decision-making down to the lowest level possible.

Distributed System
(6 Decision-making Minds)

Centralized System
(1 Decision-making Mind)

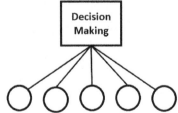

In a distributed system, more minds are engaged. The highest-level minds set the guardrails via core values and objectives (the leadership model). Each successive level customizes their objectives and their approach within those guardrails. Each level of management strives to use the minds and hands of its team, which is the next level down.

Building distributed systems has several benefits over centralized systems.

Local Information

If decision-making is distributed, decisions are made by leveraging local information. This is the information collected by team members who directly interact with the client or market. Those teams that are closest in proximity to that information are the ones making decisions. In a centralized system, however, team members pass along the local information, hoping that it will be taken into consideration by the central decision-makers. In a large and centralized organization, some of the local information may not be taken into account.

Recency

In a distributed system, decision-making is done using the most recent information because of the close proximity to that information. Decisions can often be made as soon as the information is collected. In a centralized system, you pass along local information and await a decision, one which may not fully consider all of the information received and could delay taking action.

Innovation

When decision-making is distributed, your organization will be more innovative. More minds will be working on challenges and opportunities. A key responsibility of the highest-level managers is to identify best practices created by local decision-makers and make them available to other local decision-makers. In my experience, local decision-makers make it their job to stay connected to each other in order to be on the lookout for innovation that they can leverage on their own teams. In a centralized system, innovation is limited to a smaller set of minds. Even if there is a centralized team dedicated to innovation, that team struggles to understand and consider all of the local information.

Division of Labor

When decision-making is distributed, the way you organize your teams can be more specialized. Local teams will strive to focus on what they do best and outsource what they can. This is another form of the innovation benefit. If you are working in a centralized system, you rely on the central body to determine the division of labor. However, that central body has poor access to local information, which includes knowing what the local teams do best.

Efficiency

Distributed decision-making drives efficiency. Innovation means that more efficient methods will be developed and shared. There are some who think that efficiency is an advantage of a centralized system because they can avoid reinventing the wheel. While local teams of a distributed system can sometimes duplicate efforts in performing common tasks, the increased efficiency related to innovation far outweighs the potential for savings from enforcing standards mandated by a centralized system. If local teams are required to follow a set procedure, they will be far less likely to see more efficient alternatives.

Engagement
Distributed decision-making encourages deeper engagement across your organization. This was implied in each of the previous benefits. When you leverage your team's minds and hands, they will be more engaged.

Direct Action
Finally, distributed decision-making encourages more direct action. When local teams are responsible for making their own decisions, they will take more initiative and be more accountable. In a centralized system, local teams wait for headquarters to solve problems. Even when they advocate for solutions, their action is indirect because they have to appeal to a higher authority.

 Distributed Warfare *(Leadership Example)*
War and armies are analogies frequently used for leadership. In fact, if you look at the traditional company organizational structure, it was modeled after how armies were organized in the past. Strong headquarters issued detailed battle plans to their armies in the field. Modern armies, however, are organized differently. America may have started that trend.

Think about the American revolution. The British stood in compact rows taking orders from their few commanders. The Americans were hiding behind rocks and trees and were constantly on the move. That was a major factor in how an inferior military force defeated what was considered the most formidable army of the time. Today, armies in the field have much more autonomy over their battle plan. They have freedom to adjust their tactics based on local information, as long as they remain consistent with the overall objectives. Units as small as a few soldiers have tremendous discretion in their decision-making. Distributed systems have taken over military organization, and modern companies like Google have been doing the same.

Building a distributed system may sound intimidating. You might think that you have no idea how to go about it. You do, but you just do not realize it.

Strategic Management Routines

Preparing for and practicing strategic pauses within strategic management routines is leadership with a focus on the future. You could think of strategic management as a fourth level of the strategic pause.

Strategic management is a system of nineteen management routines. These practices are on the conceptual level. Their form, when put into practice, depends on many factors, including organizational structure, key performance indicators, and personal preferences. The routines should be explicit, simple, and actionable. The form you choose is how you make them your own. For this reason, I have resisted sharing many specific examples. For instance, we will discuss team all-hands meetings and why they are important, but not specific agendas and formats. That is for you to figure out. It is your opportunity to put your signature on it. The fact that the routines are carried out is more important than their actual form.

Strategic management applies to all levels. At the organization level, these mechanisms can be seen in place for a company or division. At the team level, they are executed on the account or functional group level. Strategic management also applies to the individual. Many of these routines can also be put into practice on a personal level. For example, you should know your core strengths, the impact you have, and your vision. You should be taking a strategic pause to set objectives, which is your strategic planning, on at least an annual basis. You should be compiling a personal status, whether it has been asked for or not, and you should be striving to quantitatively measure how you are doing. Ideally, strategic management practices should be in place on every level of an organization.

The Framework
Strategic management has a simple framework with three sections, which represent a manager's three main responsibilities.

- **PLANNING:** Setting objectives. This can be done using varying timeframes. It includes tuning and adjusting objectives and determining a strategy for how you will empower and align your team and organization to those objectives.

- **MANAGEMENT:** Overseeing tactics and operations that are aligned to your strategy. Management is making your strategy real by driving routines that empower and align your team and organization.

- **MEASUREMENT:** Objectively assessing your results. This is done by grading out your objectives, strategy, and people management. This is the feedback loop that enables you to continuously improve.

Now that we have the simple framework, we will fill it in. You will see many principles and methods that we have already mentioned in one form or another.

Strategic Management

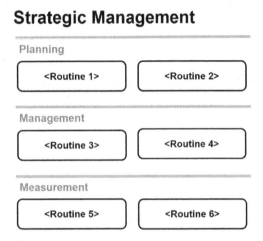

Planning
There are seven strategic management practices that fall under planning.

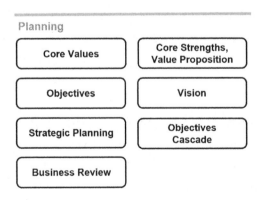

Core Values

Refer back to *Core Values* in *Foundation* (Part 3.3). Determining simple and explicit core values and living by them is the foundation of your culture. They are the minimum requirement and should be shared by everyone on your team.

Core Strengths, Value Proposition

Refer back to *Empowerment* in *Principles* (Part 3.4). Your value proposition is how you apply your core strengths to drive results for external clients or internal stakeholders. Remember that this can be applied to organizations, teams, and individuals.

It is important for both you and your team to understand the value proposition. It should be explicit, simple, and actionable. Once it is explicitly understood, everyone can seek to reinforce and deepen it and also to make sure that it is never placed at risk. In many cases, core strengths will be the value proposition. This is especially true on the individual level. The value proposition is not aspirational. It reflects current core strengths.

 Value Propositions *(Leadership Example)*
For multiple years, the value proposition of my account servicing a large bank was "Reliable, Flexible, and Scalable." If asked, every member of the team could recite this. They also took it into account in their day-to-day. We quantified it within the scorecard with metrics related to on-time delivery and change request throughput. The scorecard will be covered further in the *Measurement* section.

On an individual level, "Be a Positive Force" is part of my personal value proposition. I list this principle in *Differentiators* (Part 3.6).

Objectives

In *Strategic Alignment* (Part 3.4.2), we covered the importance of having objectives. When setting objectives, there are three guidelines you should follow.

- **VIVID:** Make your objectives as descriptive as possible. If your team can visualize the destination, their reticular activating systems will get behind the effort and they will both consciously and subconsciously be tuned to those objectives.

- **TWO TO FIVE:** Have two to five objectives. More than five can lower the probability of progressing on any of them. There is a lot of science that reinforces this point. Having fewer objectives keeps you focused.

- **DELIVERY AND GROWTH:** Set objectives that focus on the value you add today, as well as the value you hope to add in the future. Set objectives that focus on continuous improvement of delivery, which is causally related to reinforcing and deepening your current value proposition. In addition, set objectives that focus on growing your business. "Upsell" and "cross-sell" are objectives that articulate the two primary categories of growth. Up-sell is doing more of what you do today by better leveraging the products or services already being utilized. Cross-sell is providing new products or services. Another objective is "value add." This includes things like thought leadership and incremental offerings, at low or no cost, to increase satisfaction with existing offerings and prepare the client for future growth opportunities.

Building on the "value add" topic, if your objectives from the previous period were successful, you may be able to add to your value proposition. Becoming more valuable to your external client or internal stakeholders should always be the goal.

I set objectives professionally and personally on an annual basis. It is the most common timeframe. Refer to "Set Vivid Vision & Objectives" in *Strategic Alignment* (Part 3.4.2) for examples of objectives.

Vision

Vision overlaps with objectives. The difference is that vision has a longer-term timeframe and a higher-level goal. I set vision on the three- to five-year timeframe. Your annual objectives are aligned to your vision. If your vision has a three-year timeframe, achieving your annual objectives over the next three years should achieve your vision.

Loyalty Objectives and Vision *(Leadership Example)*
My teams built and ran the credit card loyalty platforms for a number of financial institutions. The objectives and visions for these teams were similar. The typical vision was "Increase Program Membership by 33% by 20XX." The objectives included with the vision looked like "Integrate with Amazon by the end of Q3" and "Implement Points Sharing with <Store specific> Program by End of Year." Achieving these objectives would increase program member engagement and enhance the value of the program, which would then attract new members to ultimately achieve the vision.

Strategic Planning

Strategic planning is the assessment of your current status, setting objectives and vision, and laying out the path to get there. The outputs are the four previous strategic management practices of core values through vision.

This method starts with assessing your previous value proposition, scorecard (which we will cover in the *Measurement* section), objectives, and vision. You may also assess your core values and core strengths, but they are less likely to change because they reflect who you are. Your value proposition will also remain fairly consistent. However, if you successfully achieved your objectives in the previous period, you may add to your value proposition. You tune your scorecard based on how your client's or stakeholders' definition of business success has changed. You will set new objectives, and your vision may be tuned but stay directionally the same.

This practice requires an impartial analysis focused outside of your team and organization. What is happening in your market? How is your competition doing and how are they changing their strategy? What best practices can you mimic?

I frequently use a SWOT (Strength, Weaknesses, Opportunities, and Threats) analysis to take my team leaders through the process. I ask them to fill out their own SWOT in advance. The "SW" are focused internally, identifying strengths and weaknesses. The "OT" are focused externally, identifying opportunities and threats. There are many leadership templates and books written about setting objectives and strategy. I strongly encourage you to learn more about the process. You will find leadership templates that appeal to your way of leading and are best suited to your space.

Another important part of strategic planning is focusing

on the state of the team. Run lots of scenarios and ask lots of questions. Who are your stars? Do they feel appreciated? Who is struggling and why? Are there any single points of failure? What is your succession plan? What are the engagement and attrition rates?

 Top-down and Bottom-up Strategy *(Leadership Template)*
Strategy originates from two possible directions.

Top-down strategy starts with the identification of an opportunity in the market. It is articulating some unfulfilled need. For example, Uber recognized that the internet enabled the creation of a ride sharing market that could be accessed from your phone.

Bottom-up strategy starts with the identification of under-leveraged assets. In ESA terms, it is articulating your core strength and value proposition and then seeking economic application of those strengths. An example would be a laptop manufacturer having excess capacity and deciding to build smart home thermostats in addition to laptops.

The ideal situation is when top-down and bottom-up strategies meet in the middle. This means there is a clear gap in the market and you have the assets that can be aligned to fill that gap.

Apply this leadership template to your business. What are the emerging or missed gaps in your market and adjacent ones? Where else can your value proposition be leveraged?

Trend Progression Strategy *(Leadership Template)*
This leadership template is going deeper into the top-down strategy discussed above. Brainstorm the big trends in the economy and the world and dig into them to generate insights. Examine those insights to uncover needs. See if you can match the needs to your value proposition or to a value proposition that you can create with your core strengths and assets. If you can match need to value proposition, set objectives and create a plan to build a business.

An example would be in-home elder-care services. The trend is a growing aging population. The insight is that this population is going to need some level of assisted living, and a percentage of them will choose to "age in place," for which they will need in-home assistance. This is especially true after the 2020 COVID-19 pandemic, when outside care facilities were disproportionally affected. If you have access to a mobile, moderately-skilled workforce, this asset could be applied to in-home assisted-living services. This is a very fast-growing market.

Objectives Cascade

Refer back to "Cascade Vision & Objectives" in *Strategic Alignment* (Part 3.4.2). Cascading objectives and vision are central to ESA.

Once the strategy is set, you and your leaders cascade it into the team. Your team delivers the value to your clients or stakeholders and they need to know the objectives and strategy to make it happen. Ideally, the cascade process is performed by each team. If they set their own objectives, they are much more likely to own them.

The cascade includes handing off metrics related to the value proposition and ultimately the scorecard. Ideally, the person who has the greatest impact on each metric should be responsible for it. They should be the named owner. Like objectives, this will increase their engagement in protecting and deepening the value proposition and delivering to the scorecard.

Business Review

Performing a business review means checking on the objectives and strategy to assess progress. This is the time to tune and adjust them based on changes at the client level, in your organization, and in the market. This is a compact version of strategic planning that is often conducted on a quarterly basis.

You may determine that an objective has been completed, or you may find that it has been rendered irrelevant or impossible to achieve. It is critical that the team sees objectives as realistic and achievable. They must be able to see a path toward completion, even if reaching it is a stretch. This is the time to make critical adjustments to that end.

The business review is also the best time to run scenarios, similar to strategic planning. Refer to "Be Ready" within *Personal Organization* (Part 3.3.2). This is a tabletop exercise of hypothetical situations. With this process, you may uncover a risk that is important enough to justify taking immediate action. Or you may isolate an opportunity that you can capitalize on before it disappears or is seized by your competition.

The business review has been manifested in professional services as the Quarterly Business Review (QBR). The QBR should be conducted both externally with your clients and internally with your stakeholders.

The form the business review takes can vary widely; there is no perfect format. Similar to the primary benefit of maintaining a status, the most important aspect of the business review is that you are taking a strategic pause. You are bringing your leadership team together, lifting your heads up from the day-to-day, and making sure you are heading in the right direction.

Management

Management is comprised of eight strategic management practices.

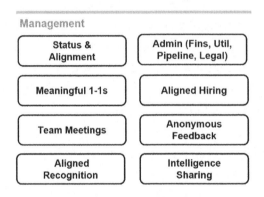

Status & Alignment

Many leaders do not like status reporting and status meetings. That is because they are not viewing them from the right perspective.

Status is more important than you think. You will recall from the "Be Ready" section in *Personal Organization* (Part 3.3.2) that keeping a status up to date enables you to be ready. Many view statuses as an update on your organization, team, and work queue for the powers that be. While this is important because it enables you to control the narrative, it is secondary to the main benefit. The primary benefit is that status is a built-in strategic pause that allows you to assess the "state of the state" of your organization, team, and work queue. Routinely assessing your status forces you to update your metrics, reflect on opportunities and risks, and check alignment to the bigger objectives. You take the pulse of the team and validate your top priorities. Because of this, everyone, regardless of whether or not it has been requested, should be pulling together a status on a biweekly or monthly basis. This is true for both the report and the meeting routine.

Similar to strategic planning, the form of your status can vary widely. How many key performance indicators (KPIs) are you tracking? Is your strategy's emphasis more on growth or delivery? Is it in the form of a PowerPoint presentation or a three-page document? Whatever form your status takes, it should be as simple as possible. This will maximize the probability that the information will be understood.

If you manage a team, you manage their workflow. You help them set priorities. There should be significant overlap between your status and the workflow management of the team. Setting priorities for their work queues overlaps with their alignment to the team's objectives. This is a critical component of your status and staff meetings. Beyond workflow management, you should be requiring them to take strategic pauses to ensure that they are aligned to the bigger objectives.

Admin

Every organization has procedures and tools they use to manage to key metrics. Since the key metrics drive decision-making, as a leader you should become an expert at using those tools, and you should customize them to the needs of your particular team and organization. If key metrics are missing, proactively add them to your status mechanism to increase their exposure and to advocate broader adoption of them. Procedures and tools typically fall into four areas:

- **FINANCIALS:** Know the financials of your business. Revenue, margin, and cash flow are the most common. Know which direction the financials are trending and know where your business stands compared to the rest of the organization. Knowing how your business and team impact the financials is also known as "business acumen."

- **UTILIZATION:** Know if you are getting the most out of your team and resources. Billable hours and billable percentage of total time are the most common metrics. If you do not think they accurately represent the yield of your team, you should also track the metrics that do. For example, strategy and analytics projects can bring in revenue on their own. However, for professional services companies, they open the door for much larger services relationships, which have value well beyond the revenue associated with the strategy and analytics work.

- **PIPELINE:** Growth is always important. The pipeline is the best indicator of growth. It is the listing of sales opportunities and where they sit in the selling process. Be up to date on upsell and cross-sell opportunities. Some opportunities are early stage while others are close to a decision by the prospect. Some opportunities are greater in value while others are smaller projects. The pipeline helps you decide how to align your resources as well as forecast future resource needs.

- **LEGAL:** Know the status of the contracts that your business maintains. A renewal should never sneak up on you. Keeping your legal house in order eliminates distractions.

Your status should include headline-level information from your administrative routines.

Meaningful One-on-ones

Many surveys on why people leave jobs report consistent results. Numbers two and three on those surveys sometimes flip-flop, but they remain the same. They are "more money" and "greater challenge." The number one reason never changes. It is "the manager." The good news is that the manager is also the reason people stay in their jobs, despite other challenges. The manager-associate relationship is the most important relationship on your team and in your organization. Meaningful one-on-ones dramatically impact this relationship. In particular, two practices will make a difference.

The first is ensuring that one-on-ones regularly occur. They are scheduled and rarely canceled. Rescheduling them is acceptable, but it should not become a habit. I am appalled when I hear someone say, "I have not talked to my manager since my review last year," or "Our one-on-ones are on the calendar, but they usually get canceled." The easiest way to tell an associate that they are not important is to not meet with them on a regular basis. For this reason, one-on-ones are mandatory. My personal preference is to meet every other week. Your organization and team may justify another level of frequency, though I recommend that it never be less than monthly.

The second practice is holding additional meaningful one-on-ones on at least a quarterly basis. This shifts the one-on-one discussion from a check-in and status conversation to a personally meaningful discussion. Doing this allows you to discuss four important topics:

- **RESULTS & RECOGNITION:** If the associate delivered an impactful result, make sure to acknowledge it. If the result is in alignment with the bigger objectives and the value proposition, recognize it more emphatically to reinforce that desired behavior.

- **OBJECTIVES, ALIGNMENT, & CAREER PATH:** Check in on the associate's individual objectives. Are they making progress? Do they need a nudge? Do they need to adjust their objectives? Are their career objectives parallel or even overlapping with their business objectives? Is there an opportunity for greater alignment?

- **PROFESSIONAL DEVELOPMENT & INTROSPECTION:** Overlapping with career path, is your associate evolving professionally? Are they getting better at leveraging their core strengths? Are they compensating for their core weaknesses? Are they addressing a non-innate blind spot that is holding them back? Do they understand their core strengths and weaknesses to the point that they put themselves in situations where they can do what they do best every day? See "Empowerment Evolution" in *Empowerment* (Part 3.4.1) for a refresher on the topic of self-empowerment.

- **PERFORMANCE EVALUATION & MUTUAL FEEDBACK:** No aspect of the associate's performance should be a surprise in their annual review. If they are doing well and exceeding expectations, you should be recognizing them in regular one-on-ones. If they are struggling in any area, you should be sharing constructive feedback and working with them to address the concern. At the same time, you should be asking them if they are getting what they need from you. You should also be asking them how you are performing and if you have exhibited any behavior that is detrimental to them or the team.

If you are conducting meaningful one-on-ones, then your associate has to say "yes" when they are asked the question, "Does your manager care about you?" You are effectively removing the number one reason people leave jobs. Further, you may even be giving them a reason to stay.

Aligned Hiring

You have isolated and articulated your team's core values and core strengths. Doing this reinforces your culture and your value proposition. Make sure that new team members share these qualities.

Aligned hiring ensures that your team will retain those core values and strengths over time as the composition of the team changes and grows. I sometimes refer to aligned hiring as "select believers."

It is tempting to be excited about a candidate because they have a particular skill or experience that is desperately needed. In these circumstances, you will be tempted to overrule your gut when it tells you something is wrong. As I shared in the "Ignoring my Gut and the Project Manager" leadership example in *Core Values* (Part 3.3.1), when a candidate checks all the boxes on paper but you still have a nagging sense that something is not quite right, it may be because they are not aligned to your core values. You should dig deeper to identify why the fit does not feel right.

There are many ways in which you can evaluate a candidate's alignment to the core values and core strengths. Some companies take it to the extreme by running candidates through detailed testing. Figure out what works for your team and organization.

Having explicit and simple core values and core strengths, and reminding interviewees that these are important concerns, is usually enough to flush out trouble.

Team Meetings

All-hands meetings are the primary way to bring your team together. At these team meetings, you and your leaders will share the "state of the state." How is the team tracking toward the bigger objectives? What are the current opportunities and risks? What are the updates from the larger organization? Make it a practice to record your all-hands meetings and make them available for those who missed the live meeting or for those who would like to revisit a topic. Your meetings can take many forms and will evolve based on feedback from your team and as a result of how the business is changing. You may occasionally substitute a team email for an in-person meeting to provide updates. However, an email alone will never hold as much weight. Sending along a short video message with the email will have greater impact.

Culture building is another form of team meeting. Getting the team out of the office to volunteer or to share a meal strengthens the culture. The form and frequency of these culture-building events depends on your situation and creativity.

Anonymous Feedback

Does your team have a mechanism to safely share feedback? My current preference is anonymous online surveys. Every other month, I collect anonymous questions and feedback. I respond to all input and share it with the team, though I modify the original submitted content if it is particularly sensitive. Sometimes it includes specific names or clues pointing to individuals. If I edit the input content, I strive to preserve the spirit of the feedback and not temper the sentiment. This practice has uncovered communication gaps with our senior-most leaders and drawn attention to unjust situations. Responding to anonymous feedback can be tricky, though. Some responses may have to be approved by HR and even legal. If I cannot answer a question, I acknowledge it and commit to determining the best response or course of action. If a team member asks for a particular action that is not a priority, I explain why and add it to my list for future consideration (my "Later/Maybe" list). This routine has been worth the investment. Having such a practice in place has deepened my credibility as a leader and says good things about the organization as a whole.

Aligned Recognition

If you strive to lead, recognition is an important part of your role. When your team delivers exceptional results, do you acknowledge their accomplishment? Many leaders just move on to the next challenge, especially if they are very busy. If the results are aligned to the core values, core strengths, value proposition, or team objectives, recognition is even more important. Applaud the aligned behavior as an example to the rest of the team. This will encourage them to take strategic pauses and to go above and beyond in order to take paths that will have greater impact on the big picture. How you recognize their accomplishment is up to you. I like to do it in our all-hands meetings. Recognition may come from corporate recognition mechanisms, but just because it is administered by corporate does not mean you should not also trumpet the good news. Finally, strive to deliver the recognition as close to the accomplishment as possible.

Intelligence Sharing

Since your management system is a distributed system, you have many minds overcoming challenges and taking advantage of opportunities. Do not leave it up to word of mouth to disseminate new intelligence across your team. Put an explicit and simple intelligence sharing mechanism in place. There are numerous ways to do this. You can create and encourage the use of a knowledge base. You can have innovators present their findings in all-hands meetings. You can hold meetings dedicated to sharing insights. Put something in place and then experiment with it. If you read any case studies of innovative organizations, you will learn about their intelligence sharing practices. If your intelligence sharing mechanism has been in place for some time, it may be worth modifying it to make it feel new. Since it captures new creativity and innovation, it should also have that feel.

Measurement

The remaining four of the nineteen strategic management routines fall under measurement.

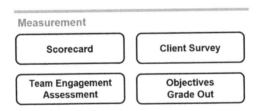

Scorecard

The scorecard is the quantification of your value proposition. It is assigning metrics to how your offering impacts your client's or stakeholders' business. Too often, the scorecard is limited to lower-level metrics, steps removed from true business impact. Do not be afraid to make the scorecard harder on your team. There are clear benefits to having it measure true business success.

When you are in agreement with your external client or internal stakeholders on how to define business success in terms of key performance indicators (KPIs), your team is immediately in a stronger long-term position. You will have transformed the relationship from being subjective and qualitative to being objective and quantitative. You can build of a clear track record of successes that will not be easily forgotten, and you will be less likely to be judged by a single issue that may have arisen. If your client or stakeholders were to claim that everything about your offering was a failure, you can use the scorecard as evidence that that particular issue was the exception rather than the rule.

 What is left in the tank? *(Leadership Example)*

For one of our financial services clients, the uptime/availability of the analytics and campaign platforms was business critical. If our client could not access those platforms, they would not be able to extract the intelligence needed to make marketing decisions, or to act on those marketing decisions by executing campaigns. We agreed to a metric of 99 percent platform availability. Because we effectively cascaded those metrics into the team, we always knew what was left in the uptime tank. In other words, we knew how much more time the platform could be unavailable before we missed that KPI. There were many instances where we modified our approach to updating operating systems and software so that there would be minimal impact on availability because we knew where we stood at that moment.

Client Survey

Whether your clients or stakeholders are external or internal, it is important to directly solicit their feedback regarding topics such as satisfaction and advocacy. I personally prefer measuring advocacy. The willingness to recommend your products or services to others has been established by many as the most important metric. Refer back to the "100% Client Advocacy" leadership example in *Strategic Alignment* (Part 3.4.2). You should be asking for specifics on what is going well and what is missing the mark. Your client is ultimately the reason your business exists. Typically, organizations issue formal client surveys on an annual basis. You should also leverage the business review process to collect this feedback, something that is usually done quarterly. As a rule, you should be on the lookout for client feedback during every interaction.

Team Engagement Assessment

Team engagement has a direct impact on the value you deliver to your clients or stakeholders. It is reflected in virtually every metric, including satisfaction and advocacy, revenue, margin, and attrition. You should also measure team engagement because it is your opportunity to get feedback on your team's leadership, which includes your own leadership. There are many approaches to capturing this feedback; Gallup's Q12 engagement survey is particularly well respected. Many large companies have organization-wide associate engagement surveys. If they are well designed, a subset of the results that includes only your team may be available. When a corporate mechanism such as this does exist, it presents an excellent opportunity to compare the leadership of your team to that of the larger organization.

Objectives Grade Out

You have set objectives for growth and delivery. These objectives should include some connection to the scorecard, client survey, and team engagement assessment. The scores attained on those measurement mechanisms are relevant objectives themselves. Your team has cascaded those objectives into their own objectives. It is important to report progress toward the bigger objectives on a regular basis. It is not enough to roll them out and assess them at the end of the year. If the team understands where they are on track and where they are falling behind, they can take strategic pauses and adjust their behavior accordingly. If an objective no longer applies or a new one becomes clear, the team needs to know. You can grade out your objectives in many different ways. I report out on the associated metric and then assign a red, yellow, or green grade. Red means we are off-track and dramatic action is required. Yellow means we are behind and additional actions will be needed to catch up. Green means we are on track and should keep doing what we are doing. Note that I recommended the same grade out approach in "Evolution via Red, Yellow, Green" in *Leadership Model Evolution* (Part 3.1) as a way to assess your progress in evolving your personal leadership model.

Populated Framework *(Strategic Management Artifact)*

Below is the strategic management framework with all nineteen routines included.

Strategic Management

Planning

Core Values	Core Strengths, Value Proposition
Objectives	Vision
Strategic Planning	Objectives Cascade
Business Review	

Management

Status & Alignment	Admin (Fins, Util, Pipeline, Legal)
Meaningful 1-1s	Aligned Hiring
Team Meetings	Anonymous Feedback
Aligned Recognition	Intelligence Sharing

Measurement

Scorecard	Client Survey
Team Engagement Assessment	Objectives Grade Out

Transactional to Systematic

Managers who do not leverage a strategic management approach operate in a transactional world. They only lead in the present. By practicing strategic pauses, they strive to make decisions that challenge business as usual and align to core strengths and the larger objectives. However, their progress is largely influenced by which situations come into their view.

When you embrace strategic management, you are shifting to a systematic approach. You are placing waypoints in front of your team. These waypoints are the strategic management routines that are designed to make the principles of empowerment and strategic alignment real. You are no longer relying on the right situations coming across your desk. As outlined in opening of this part, strategic management is leadership focused on the future. It is setting up moments in the future that you prepare for and take strategic pauses within when they arrive.

When you treat the strategic management routines as mandatory, you show your team that you have a plan. You set clear expectations as to how the team will run. It is your operating model. If you are not consistently performing these routines, they will see them as passing fads and their impact will be compromised.

As situations arise, you will refer to the strategic management routines more and more. For example, escalations that were previously handled transactionally and in isolation now have a proper forum. If one of your leaders comes to you with an emerging risk, instead of remediating the risk as a stand-alone project, you ask the leader to raise the concern with the rest of the team leaders in the upcoming status meeting. That both informs them of the risk and engages them in the remediation, which, as a result, will likely be stronger than if it had been addressed by fewer minds outside of a strategic management routine.

Once strategic management is established, the team's reliance on you lessens and their reliance on the system increases. Previously, they needed you to weigh in on any decision impacting the big picture. With strategic management, they can predict your response. Even better, they will realize that their own response is equivalent to what yours would have been. Situations that previously looked gray to your team are now black and white. See "Transforming Gray into Black and White" in *How do you build a personal leadership model?* (Part 1.7).

 Beware of Compliance *(Leadership Template)*
I am not talking about the compliance or regulatory department. I am talking about how your team will characterize your rollout and oversight of strategic management. Will they see you as just "checking the boxes?" Or will they see you as instituting and executing a plan that will drive the team and business forward?

An example of what this leadership template is trying to avoid is when companies put strategic business planning in place for teams whose business has growth potential. The planning is filled with impactful exercises that can greatly promote growth. In my experience, such strategic planning has a positive impact on growth only when the team remains focused. In rolling out the planning, companies tend to ask too much of the teams in short periods of time. They see the value of all the aspects of the planning and want it all in place as soon as possible. When teams struggle to integrate the new approach, the company's response is to increase the pressure. Very quickly, the strategic planning turns into a compliance exercise; if a team does not get through the mandatory activities, there is punitive action. Instead of being focused on driving growth, the teams are focused on not being called out. The intent of strategic planning is now compromised by the all-at-once rollout. The better approach is to phase in the strategic planning by having the teams focus on two or three aspects each quarter instead of everything immediately.

Rollout by Impact

Putting nineteen strategic management routines in place at once is not realistic. If you try to do this, you will definitely be seen as "checking the boxes."

Take a phased approach. Identify which routines will have the greatest impact and make them part of the first phase. At the same time, share the entire strategic management landscape with your team. Lay out the intended future phases so they know what to expect.

Putting strategic management in place is a team objective in itself. Grade out the progress like any other objective. On the next page is a snapshot of my red, yellow, and green grade out of the financial services and insurance division's operating model for strategic management. I called it "The FSI Way."

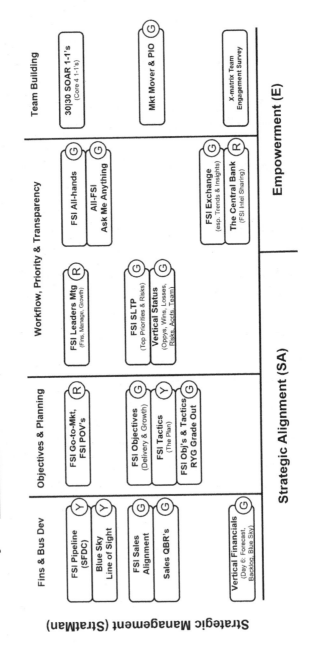

The FSI Way >> Vertical-level w/RYG Grade Out

You will note that "Vertical-level" is underlined because there was an "Account-level" version that my account leaders were putting in place. Also note that the framework is slightly different than what was previously shown. This is an example of customizing the strategic management framework to the team. You can see that it is still directionally the same.

NOT Optional

Strategic management is largely doing what we already know we should be doing. Too often, we allow our daily scramble to get in the way. We behave as if these routines are optional. If you strive to lead, they are not. Leadership means staying on message and making sure you execute all of these strategic management routines.

Strategic management is mandatory. Yes, there will be situations that conflict with your all-hands or your one-on-ones. It is not always necessary, however, to drop everything to deal with them. Sometimes it is appropriate to push back on a distraction. This will eliminate the expectation that you are always at someone's beck and call. Rescheduling these meetings is acceptable but cancelling rarely is. Making sure your strategic management routines happen shows your team that the routines are important.

Many in management positions allow these routines to be optional. As a manager, you should set up a system that ensures consistency. Some may view this as "checking the boxes," so pour yourself and your personality into each of them. If you are not invested, your team will feel it. You will find that following through on strategic management routines quickly sets you apart.

I often say that leadership is boring. You may sometimes feel like your team all-hands meetings and one-on-ones are uninspiring. They mean more to your team than you realize. Again, this is especially true if you are among the few people in your environment who are committed to these routines. In good times, your strategic management helps drive the team and business forward. In bad times, it becomes the mooring they tie off to as they weather the storm. Yes, strategic management can feel boring. The sustainable results supported by strategic management are far from that.

THINKING QUESTIONS

▸ How would you describe your current leadership/management system/operating model?

▸ Do you treat your management routines as mandatory, or do you allow them to be put on the backburner by the daily whirlwind?

▸ Are there routines that you manage like a centralized system that should be a distributed system?

▸ What do you think is the most important thing you do as a leader? Is it codified as a practice?

Artifact: Below is the ESA grid with *The Strategic Pause* and *Strategic Management* methods filled in.

ESA

"Know how you impact the big picture"

	Foundation (Operational)	Present (Tactical)	Future (Strategic)
Principles	**Core Values** • Mutual Respect • Work Ethic • Responsibility • Integrity • Credibility	**Empowerment (E)** • Max Strengths, Min Weaknesses • "Do what you do best every day"	**Strategic Alignment (SA)** • Set Vivid Vision & Objectives • Cascade Vision & Objectives – Create a "line of sight"

Methods	**Personal Organization**
	• Build an External Mind
	• Be Ready: Status,
	   Run Scenarios
	• The Power of Little Habits
		The Strategic Pause
		• Be Cool & Composed
		• Take Initiative &
		   Challenge the BAU
		• Align to Core & Objectives
			Strategic Management
			• Build a Distributed System
			• NOT Optional

Differentiators			

3.6 Differentiators

The principles are the "what." The methods are the "how." The differentiators are the "who."

The primary principles and methods are fundamental. It is difficult to argue that any of them should be swapped out for different principles or methods. This is why I sometimes refer to them as "self-evident truths." You make them your own by rephrasing them in your own words. There is more room for variation with differentiators.

Differentiators are the chief way you make your personal leadership model your own. They are the principles and methods in your set of core strengths that apply to leadership. Think of your differentiators as your leadership style. They support and amplify the primary principles and methods.

We will cover three differentiators that reflect my personal leadership style. If they are part of your strengths, consider including them in your differentiators as they have a big impact on leadership. That said, this is where you put your signature on your personal leadership model. Pick differentiators that reflect who you are. Do not be afraid to ask your team, peers, manager, and friends for their feedback. Examples of differentiators that differ from the three I will describe include being inspiring, tenacious, likable, empathetic, innovative, a future thinker, in command, a quick learner, and adaptable. Overlapping with "Introspection" in *Empowerment* (Part 3.4.1), there are numerous resources that can help you isolate your differentiators.

3.6.1 **Be a Positive Force**

Positive people stand out. We like being around them. I am talking about positive people who acknowledge the negative but choose to focus on the positive.

You can control whether you are a positive or negative person. It is easy to see the negative in people and situations. To a certain extent, it is how we are wired. It is tied to survival: we automatically see the negative, the risk.

I am not making the case that you should ignore the negative. It should be a factor in your decision-making, but it should not be the foundation. Being positive takes more effort; it requires moving beyond the negative. Sometimes, the negative will outweigh the positive and you will be forced to find a silver lining.

Being a positive force starts with accepting reality. Whatever happened has happened. The question is, how do you proceed? Do you trudge forward with a bad attitude or do you drive forward and make the best of the situation? That is your choice. I am not advocating wearing rose-colored glasses; you can be realistic and still be positive.

To reinforce my point, whom would you rather be around and work with? Most will choose being around positive people. I would rather be in a tough situation working with positive people than in a good situation with coworkers who have a bad attitude. The latter starts out in a better place, but the former will probably have a better outcome. At the very least, it will be less stressful and more enjoyable.

There are books, services, and industries dedicated to the power of being positive. Many of them cite the science that proves that being positive has an impact. I recommend reading some of them.

There are two practices that I believe drive being a positive force.

Enthusiasm, Optimism, Humor

Being a positive force is about attitude. It is striving to exhibit three qualities:

- **ENTHUSIASM:** Display your enthusiasm. If you feel excited about something, express it. If you sense that a situation needs positive energy, inject some. Others will join in. In some cases, you may be teased about it, but the teasing itself is positive energy.

- **OPTIMISM:** Every situation has positives and negatives. Which do you choose to focus on and use as your basis for moving forward? Adopting an optimistic attitude makes the most trying circumstances more tolerable or even enjoyable. It will make it more likely that others will focus on a positive outcome.

- **HUMOR:** Humor reduces stress and loosens people up. Science proves that humor is good for all of us. There are some situations, however, where humor may not be appropriate. Too much of it can lower productivity, while introducing it at inappropriate times can indicate that you underestimate the seriousness of a situation. The line fluctuates and is different for every person and situation. However, humor is often welcome right up to that line. Note that I am talking about humor based on good intent. Humor based on bad intent is being passive aggressive.

Positive leaders who exhibit these qualities stand out and are likely to be more successful.

View as an Opportunity or a Challenge

Bad things happen. How do you respond when they do? Do you let them slow you down or stop you altogether? How long do you linger over them, allowing them to negatively impact your mood and behavior?

In moments of truth, leadership is obvious. Negative situations provide a clear opportunity for you to step up and drive the team forward. Start with acknowledging the situation and quickly move toward working with your team to learn what you can to remedy things, and then rally everyone to overcome the obstacles.

Be a Positive Force and Parenting *(Leadership Example)*

"Be a positive force" was a lesson my wife and I used consistently with our twin daughters. If they were fighting with each other or focusing too much on the negative aspects of a situation, we would tell them to be a positive force. Staying on message with the benefits of being positive made a difference. One of our proudest parenting moments was when we once overheard our girls having a disagreement. When the exchange started to become unproductive, one daughter reminded the other to be a positive force. It worked. It was even better when we ran into scenarios where they reminded us to be a positive force! It is part of our family culture.

Rising through the Breach *(Leadership Example)*

My company experienced a client data breach incident that left some of our clients liable. Customer personal information was stolen and could be used for illegal purposes. The remediation required weeks of long days for all of our teams. However, after acknowledging the negative aspects of the incident, we kept our teams focused on the steps toward recovery. Our leaders provided air cover by intentionally taking on the bulk of our clients' frustrations. Since we took responsibility, stayed composed, and quickly rallied our teams to remediate the situation, we found that many of our client relationships grew stronger. There is an old saying that you learn more about people in bad times than in good. Our clients' trust and belief in us deepened because of our response. The incident was a challenge that turned into an opportunity to strengthen the relationships.

THINKING QUESTIONS

▶▶ Do you have a reputation for being positive or negative? Do you hide your negativity by declaring that you are a realist?

▶▶ Do you think your team perceives you differently than you perceive yourself?

▶▶ How long do negative events impact your perspective and behavior?

▶▶ How quickly do you shift to a learning mindset when confronted with a setback?

3.6.2 Simplify

The ability to simplify may be the most valuable skill in the working world. I am not being hyperbolic. Today, we are bombarded with more information than ever before. It can take many forms, including customer feedback, data from your operations, team perspectives, market intelligence, third party assessments, etc. And it is only getting worse. This means that decision-making is becoming more and more difficult and, as a result, the ability to simplify is a clear differentiator.

If you are able to simplify, you are more likely to understand what is happening and be able to communicate that to your team. And, it means you and your team will be better able to focus on what is most important.

Why are we being bombarded with more and more information? Why do things get more complicated over time? I think there are two reasons for the explosion.

The first is that the quantity of available data is expanding exponentially. Technology is enabling much greater access to information and is also generating more data. Examples are making customer profile information available to all marketing touch-points, and location data generated by your phone as you carry it around. Getting more local and recent information regarding your customers and operations is a good thing. However, all data is not created equal. Simplification separates the impactful from the non-impactful data. Simplification boils data down so that it is understandable and actionable.

The second reason is what I call layering of process. Over time, processes naturally become more complicated. This stems from new processes or policies being layered on top of legacy processes or policies. It is much easier to put a new process in place than it is to compare it to what already exists and replace only what is needed. Another term for this layering of process is "bureaucracy." We have all experienced that. More bureaucracy means simplification is necessary. This is a root cause of why large companies adapt more slowly over time.

Being able to simplify is not an easy skill to learn. The ability is often tied to background and experience. That said, we all have the ability to do it and, given its importance, we all should be developing the skill. Strive to restate virtually every situation in the simplest terms possible. Isolate the first principles. That is how you will develop the skill. Without simplification, you will be less likely to stay focused on what is most important.

Within ESA, it simplifies (pun intended) down to two concepts.

Syntax & Semantics

As I shared earlier, "Syntax & Semantics" is the first leadership template that I use within my strategic pauses. In virtually every situation, I put it into action.

Syntax is the application or form. It is the letters, numbers, symbols, and pictures of the subject of your focus. Semantics, it follows, is the meaning or substance that is derived from the syntax. In every situation, you will be presented with syntax. Sometimes, there is little difference between the syntax and the semantics. A simple example is when someone uses words that mean exactly what they intend. However, many situations are not that straightforward. As a result, it takes a little thinking to figure out the meaning. Much of the time, more information is needed.

An example of this is when something has gone wrong and begun to escalate. First, phones, emails, and messaging are bombarded with details. Each notification concerns problems with different services provided to your client. After collecting information, you determine that the failures were caused by the marketing platform being inaccessible. After investigating further, you learn that a data center power outage brought the system down, which impacted outgoing email campaigns and the arming of all the services provided by the marketing platform. The messages received about the failures of different services was the syntax. The semantics was the platform being down due to the power outage.

Syntax and semantics are central to troubleshooting. The first step in solving any problem is isolating the root cause, the semantics. Too often, people focus on cascading impacts, which is the syntax. Dealing with lower back pain is an example of this. One response is to take a pain killer, but that would be treating the symptom. Why is your lower back sore? If the answer is that you strained it lifting boxes and you are confident that there is no long-term damage, then taking a pain killer is a proper response. In other words, you are fairly sure that you know the root cause. If you are not sure of the root cause, however, that is where your focus should be.

For greater impact, always strive to move beyond the syntax/application and get to the semantics/meaning.

Min Admin, Max Value

In your work, you should strive to minimize the time you allocate to administration and maximize the time you dedicate to adding value. As I explained earlier in this section, things naturally become more complicated than needed. Striving to simplify fights against this.

When processes are first put in place, they have a purpose. Over time, the purpose behind a process can become unclear. When that happens, the process becomes administration/bureaucracy. You still follow the process because it is policy, and it is the way you have always done it.

"Min Admin, Max Value" is the principle that purpose always comes before process. Whenever you recognize that a process is being executed for the sake of the process, take the initiative and simplify. This is closely related to the "Balance Process and Results" leadership template in *The Strategic Pause* (Part 3.5.1).

Error handling processes are a good example of this concept. When something goes wrong, you account for the possibility of facing that problem again in the future. You put a process in place to check for and handle the error. When the larger system changes, do you validate that all the error handling processes still apply? What if the source of the error-causing data was discontinued? If you do not review the processes you put in place, you will continue to execute them even though they have no purpose and add no value.

Another example is one's personal organization system. We all know people who are supremely organized. They have an elaborate system of many lists, using font variations and different pen colors, etc. They seem to be organizing all the time. They are well-intentioned, but their priority is their organization system rather than the actual work. The purpose of a personal organization system is to minimize the time organizing (administration) and maximize the time focused on the important priorities (doing something of value). Pay attention to the amount of time you spend organizing. If you are spending too much time doing it, it is time to simplify your system.

We are often too patient with bureaucracy because its costs are not fully visible. When you add up the time wasted adhering to legacy processes that have lost their connection to purpose, change is quickly justified. Management consultants often like bureaucracy because it requires less effort to identify opportunities for improvement.

Do not wait for processes to become bureaucracy before initiating change. Challenge any process that you suspect could be improved. Every second that you recapture from administration is a second that can be applied to value add. This is an application of the strategic pause's concept of taking initiative and challenging business as usual.

Connect Status with Rate of Change *(Leadership Template)*
Are your status reports and status meetings following the right cadence? If the majority of the information on your status does not change every week, then a weekly cadence does not make sense. If one-third of the updates change every other week, then biweekly is probably the right schedule. Strive to eliminate the extra administration of preparing and publishing information that has not changed since the last iteration. If you are publishing the same information, your audience will begin to tune out the update and, when you do communicate something new and important, it is more likely to be missed.

THINKING QUESTIONS

▸ Do you make things more complicated or do you simplify and bring order? What would your team and peers say?

▸ Are you pulled into situations outside of your responsibilities because you are a simplifier and can "get to the bottom of it?"

▸ When presented with an escalation, do you respond immediately, or do you strive to get a better understanding of the bigger picture?

▸ Do you write long and wordy emails when you could get the message across with a few bullet points?

3.6.3 **Be Transparent**

Like composure, transparency is one of the most cited qualities of a leader. Transparency is being willing to share more background and justification with the team than they might initially need. It may be information about the overall direction of the company or the reasoning behind your decisions. Transparency shows the team that you trust them.

Being transparent does not mean you share everything, however. As a people manager, you are trusted with information before it is ready for broader consumption. You should know where to draw the line as to how much is too much.

By being transparent, you are arming your team with more information. This is part of building a distributed system. If the team is responsible for making decisions that impact the business, they should have all the pertinent facts. When your team has a more complete picture, their feedback has more impact. You are a better decision-maker because your team is arming you with better information and alternatives. Transparency goes both ways.

Within ESA, being transparent is represented by the following two concepts.

On Message

Being transparent is staying on message. Consistency is key. If you are inconsistent, your team may not fully understand and may even wonder if there is something you are not telling them.

Being on message also means being repetitive. Use consistent language. When you set and reinforce objectives, do not vary the wording. Remember that every team has existing and new members who may not have fully understood the message. Repetition reinforces its importance.

Never miss an opportunity to reinforce alignment to the value proposition and objectives. This is especially true with wins; it is important to celebrate accomplishments. When the accomplishments reinforce the value proposition or show progress toward the objectives, it is a bigger deal. Make sure the team understands this. See "Aligned Recognition" in *Strategic Management* (Part 3.5.2).

In general, you should reinforce ties back to your leadership model. If you are striving to lead, share your leadership model with the team. When you have tangible evidence of the model working, make it known to them. At first, members of the team may tease you by throwing your leadership model terms back at you. Do not get defensive; it means they are starting to get it. That is exactly what happened with me and the strategic pause. People would ask, "Do we need a strategic pause?" to tease me when a situation needed further examination. Shortly thereafter, they were taking strategic pauses themselves.

Being transparent can be awkward, especially at first. Those who report directly to you may not be used to getting so much of the story. Explain that you believe they can handle the additional insight and that it will inform their decision-making and feedback. Explicitly say that you trust them and remind them that you are always open to feedback.

You are more likely to get pushback if you work in a technical industry. Technical practitioners are often very skeptical of management. They tend to mostly see value in terms of technical accomplishment. If you stay on message, they will eventually recognize your commitment and you will break through.

Manage to One Reality

A key responsibility of leadership is managing the perceptions of your team's different clients. When taken too far, a leader can end up managing multiple different realities. The difference between the status you report internally versus externally is a clear example. If the difference between the two stories is too great, it is only a matter of time before you slip up. When that happens, you will lose the client's trust. Being transparent has the opposite effect.

Strive to bring the multiple realities together by being more transparent with the client. Their initial reaction to getting a deeper level of information may be strong. They may be getting information that they asked for previously but were denied. They may question if you have ulterior motives. Many clients actually view flushing out the real story as their role and when they understand that it matches your status, their trust in you increases. It takes work and patience as you increase the level of transparency, but the long-term benefits of deeper trust are worth it.

There are a couple of disclaimers for "Manage to One Reality." First, you need to hold the line on confidential information. For example, profitability should not be shared with the client. Second, if your relationship is strictly supply chain or legal, achieving a deeper level of transparency may not be appropriate. It can be tricky to figure out. By starting slowly, you can determine if they will be open to greater transparency.

 Transparency in Projects *(Leadership Template)*
Transparency is a good policy during big projects and project management in general. If you are managing multiple realities, your approach to problems is to try and fix them behind the scenes. Your goal is for the client to think everything is always on track. However, the client lives in the real world. They know that big projects rarely proceed seamlessly. As a result, they will not expect their project to be the first perfect project to have zero challenges.

When you run into issues, share them with the client when appropriate. This is why risk management is a defined part of project management. But do not just share risks with them. Share your workarounds and mitigation plans as well. If, for example, a developer on the critical path leaves the company, what is the backfill plan? If there is a delay in the delivery of a key input, is there a way to mock-up the particular input so that work does not have to stop, or can the impact to the critical path be minimized by shifting resources to other tasks while you wait? My experience is that being transparent during big and trying projects deepens trust. The client feels like they were in the trenches with you. Because you share risks and workarounds, they believe that you care as much about their project as they do.

The Delayed Proposal Win *(Leadership Example)*

My team built and maintained the credit card acquisition platform for a bank that had acquired a large credit card issuer. The credit card issuer had their own acquisition platform that had been in place for almost 20 years. The bank asked for bids to consolidate to one platform and we won the bid. It was a huge win. The bank then decided to put their non-card acquisition platform out to bid, which we also won. The non-card client wanted to start right away, but we were midway through the first consolidation at the time. Given the massive amount of work left, the increased risk of taking on another integration was too high. We declined the second win and explained the high risk. Within our company, this was a controversial decision because the non-card business was worth millions of dollars.

We were told that we should take it on and figure it out. But that was not the right thing to do. Being transparent with the potential non-card client was the better approach. They were impressed. They asked when we would be ready, and we provided a timeline. The client signed a one-year extension with the legacy provider, and we were awarded the new business a year later when we had the capacity and the risk was much lower.

THINKING QUESTIONS

➤ What information are you not sharing that would benefit your team?

➤ Is your team willing to ask any question at any time?

➤ What are the three messages and objectives you should always be reinforcing?

➤ Are the realities, the statuses, that you are managing with your client and your company leadership too far apart?

Artifact: Below is the ESA grid with *Differentiators* filled in. This is the fully populated ESA leadership model.

ESA
"Know how you impact the big picture"

	Foundation (Operational)	Present (Tactical)	Future (Strategic)
Principles	**Core Values** • Mutual Respect • Work Ethic • Responsibility • Integrity • Credibility	**Empowerment (E)** • Max Strengths, Min Weaknesses • "Do what you do best every day"	**Strategic Alignment (SA)** • Set Vivid Vision & Objectives • Cascade Vision & Objectives – Create a "line of sight"
Methods	**Personal Organization** • Build an External Mind • Be Ready: Status, Run Scenarios • The Power of Little Habits	**The Strategic Pause** • Be Cool & Composed • Take Initiative & Challenge the BAU • Align to Core & Objectives	**Strategic Management** • Build a Distributed System • NOT Optional
Differentiators	**Be a Positive Force** • Enthusiasm, Optimism, Humor • View as an Opportunity or a Challenge	**Simplify** • Syntax & Semantics • Min Admin, Max Value	**Be Transparent** • On Message • Manage to One Reality

3.7 **ESA as Guardrails**

We have now covered the complete ESA leadership model. We have established the *Leadership Model Framework* and filled in the *Foundation, Principles, Methods,* and *Differentiators.* In the process, you have been building your own personal leadership model. At multiple points, I have emphasized that ESA provides the guardrails—the concepts—and you determine what form those concepts take. Put another way, ESA provides the direction, and your personal leadership model contains the details that are customized to you.

The "ESA as Guardrails" leadership template below is a summary of ESA that shows how the concepts work together and build on each other.

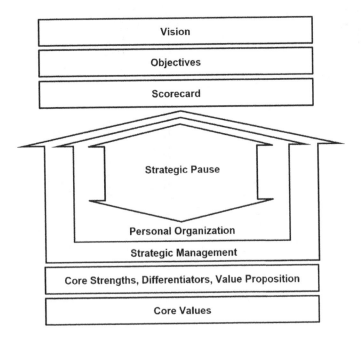

Review this artifact from the bottom up. This represents that ESA is a bottom-up distributed system. First comes *Core Values, Core Strengths,* and *Differentiators.* These are what you use to add value. When you apply your *Core Strengths* and *Differentiators,* they become your *Value Proposition.* They are your assets. This is your start.

Jump to the top of the artifact. *Vision* refers to your long-term objectives, usually three to five years out. *Objectives* are your medium-term objectives, usually one year out. The *Scorecard* is how you confirm you are staying true to your *Value Proposition,* which plays a big role in making progress toward your *Vision* and *Objectives.* These are your sustainable results. This is your finish.

Between the bottom and top are your processes. These are the systems and plan that leverage your assets to deliver your defined sustainable results. These methods are represented as arrows.

Strategic Management contains all your management routines, including your objectives cascade, all-hands meetings, meaningful one-on-ones, and team engagement surveys. Your mandatory management routines strive to leverage the bottom, the assets, and stay aligned to the top, the sustained results.

Strategic Management includes *Personal Organization.* In many ways, *Personal Organization* is strategic management at the individual level. It enables you to stay focused on what is most important, which are the activities that connect the bottom to the top.

Inside of *Personal Organization* is the *Strategic Pause.* The two-way arrow reflects your consistent validation that the decisions you make leverage both your assets and your team's, and that they are aligned to sustainable results. Within the *Strategic Pause,* you will particularly leverage your *Differentiators* as they are your strengths that make up your leadership style.

Core Values, Core Strengths, Differentiators, and Value Proposition represent Empowerment. Vision, Objectives, and the Scorecard represent Strategic Alignment. All three methods make up the processes in between Empowerment (the bottom) and Strategic Alignment (the top).

THINKING QUESTIONS

▸ Which guardrails have you been missing or not emphasizing enough?

▸ What additional insights do you gain by reformatting your personal leadership model as guardrails?

▸ Are there sections of The ESA Leadership Model (Part 3) you should revisit and think more about?

STRATEGIC
PAUSE

PART 4

Leadership Evolution

We have walked through the ESA leadership model from the ground up. We started with the *Leadership Model Framework* and moved to the *Foundation*. Next, we covered the *Principles* and the *Methods* that make them real. Finally, we closed with *Differentiators* that amplify the rest of the model and make up your leadership style. Conceptually, this is the logical path to follow. Each section builds on the previous sections. "ESA as Guardrails" summarizes how it all works together.

Your leadership journey will not follow this path exactly. In this next part, I share three leadership templates that are different leadership development paths. Where appropriate, I direct you to the relevant ESA content.

4.1 **Satisfaction via Overlap**

This simple leadership template will help guide your directional career path. It will resonate with those who are early in their careers as well as with those who are questioning their current path. Your career satisfaction can be tied to the overlap of three quick assessments: core strengths, passion, and economic value.

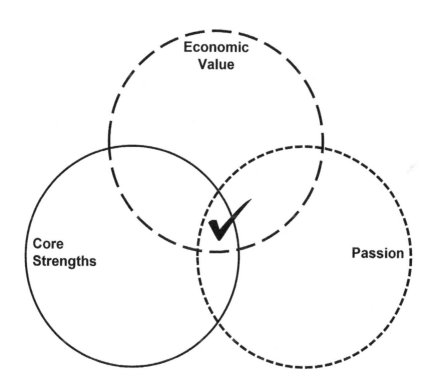

- **CORE STRENGTHS:** Do you know your core strengths? Do you do what you do best every day? If your career path is aligned to your core strengths, you will be good at your job. See *Empowerment* (Part 3.4.1).

- **PASSION:** What gets you excited? What is your purpose? If your career path is aligned to your passion, you will rarely have trouble with motivation.
  See *Strategic Alignment* (Part 3.4.2).

- **ECONOMIC VALUE:** Are you able to pay your bills? Are you able to put something away each month? If your career path provides an income that supports you and enables you to plan for the future, you have removed one of the biggest sources of stress in the world today.
  See "Value Proposition" in *Empowerment* (Part 3.4.1) and in *Strategic Management* (Part 3.5.2).

Where are you positioned in this overlap? How can you approach your current role differently to find more overlap? Do you need to make a dramatic change to your career path?

4.2 Role Evolution

As you advance through your career, you will hit multiple milestones. Each career milestone represents a change in role. Being successful in one will promote you to the next. With each new role, you will focus on different leadership principles and methods to be successful.

The "Role Evolution" leadership template lays out five career milestones and roles. It maps to the three ESA principles or methods needed for success in each role. There are more, but I list the top three. Use this leadership template to determine what to focus on to master your current role and prepare for the next.

| Individual Contributor | Subject Matter Expert | Manager | Leader | Executive |

INDIVIDUAL CONTRIBUTOR: Getting the job is the milestone. Your focus is on personal productivity and being a good team member. You are always looking for new learning opportunities. You strive to understand and exceed expectations, to add value.

- **SITUATION MANAGEMENT – BE COOL & COMPOSED:** You are a professional. This means you keep your emotions in check and base your behavior on rational factors. See *Situation Management* (Part 2.1).

- **PERSONAL ORGANIZATION:** Getting work done is why you are being paid. You are organized and prioritized. You know how to manage your time to maximize productivity. See *Personal Organization* (Part 3.3.2).

- **EMPOWERMENT – INTROSPECTION:** You isolate your core strengths and apply them to the work. You turn your core strengths into skills and acknowledge your blind spots. See *Empowerment* (Part 3.4.1).

SUBJECT MATTER EXPERT (SME): Establishing your reputation as a leader in your functional area is the milestone. Your focus is on creating and sharing best practices. People come to you for help to overcome problems and take advantage of opportunities. You train and ramp up new team members, and you strive to increase the value of the role.

- **EMPOWERMENT – CORE STRENGTHS:** Your core strengths are a good fit for the role. You leverage them as much as you can while actively plotting your career path. You are determining what skills and experiences you need to keep moving forward. See *Empowerment* (Part 3.4.1) and "Meaningful One-on-ones" in *Strategic Management* (Part 3.5.2).

- **SIMPLIFICATION:** You are the go-to person when something goes wrong. You isolate the root cause and figure out how to recover. You can explain the nuances of the role better than anyone else. See *Leadership Templates & Initiative* (Part 2.2) and *Simplify* (Part 3.6.2).

- **STRATEGIC MANAGEMENT – INTELLIGENCE SHARING:** You are asked to share your "secret sauce" in an effort to build more stars like you. You explore new approaches and technology to evolve your role and be more productive and valuable. See "Intelligence Sharing" in *Strategic Management* (Part 3.5.2).

MANAGER: Promotion to management is the milestone. You are responsible for a team. You focus on work queues, performance evaluations, professional development, and recognition. You strive to use both minds and hands. You are trying to build a team of star performers.

- **PERSONAL ORGANIZATION – TEAM WORKFLOW:** You are no longer organizing just for yourself. You are assigning and keeping track of current projects and planning for future projects. You are learning to set expectations within and outside of your team. See "Consistent Expectation Setting" in *Core Values* (Part 3.3.1), *Personal Organization* (Part 3.3.2), and *Strategic Management* (Part 3.5.2).

- **EMPOWERMENT:** You understand the strengths and weaknesses of each member of your team. You take strategic pauses when aligning work to consider those strengths and opportunities for development. You encourage introspection across your team. See *Empowerment* (Part 3.4.1) and *The Strategic Pause* (Part 3.5.1).

- **STRATEGIC MANAGEMENT – MEANINGFUL ONE-ON-ONES, STATUS & ALIGNMENT, SCORECARD, ADMIN:** You take management seriously. Meaningful one-on-ones are critical to the empowerment and alignment of your team. Your team status isolates the top priorities and risks for upper management, which is tied to the scorecard. You are becoming an expert in the administration tools centered around the organization's key metrics. See *Strategic Management* (Part 3.5.2).

LEADER: Being promoted to senior management is the milestone. You are responsible for long-term objectives that align to the company's objectives, and you ensure that your team contributes to both. Building productive managers and establishing a system are keys to your success.

- **STRATEGIC ALIGNMENT:** Your success is based on achieving your objectives. Working with your managers to set objectives and cascade them into the team is critical given that it is the team who delivers for the client or stakeholders. See *Strategic Alignment* (Part 3.4.2) and "Objectives," "Objectives Cascade," and "Strategic Planning" in *Strategic Management* (3.5.2).

- **BE TRANSPARENT:** You are on message with the objectives and value proposition. You do not shy away from difficult topics. You are your team's primary link to the larger organization and they trust you. You are building credibility. See "Status & Alignment" and "Team Meetings" in *Strategic Management* (Part 3.5.2) and *Be Transparent* (Part 3.6.3).

- **STRATEGIC MANAGEMENT – TEAM MEETINGS, INTELLIGENCE SHARING:** Your all-hands meetings build a sense of team. Each team member understands how everyone contributes to the organization's success. You strive to leverage as many minds as possible via your intelligence sharing routines. Innovations from your team have impact on the larger organization. See "Team Meetings," "Anonymous Feedback," and "Intelligence Sharing" in *Strategic Management* (Part 3.5.2).

EXECUTIVE: The career milestone is being fully responsible for your organization's strategy. The rest of the organization aligns to your objectives. You are primarily external facing so you no longer engage in day-to-day operations. You isolate the true priorities within the information deluge. You are the role model for the culture and your success depends on empowering and aligning your leaders and their systems.

- **CORE VALUES:** You set the cultural tone. You task the organization with hiring and building the ideal associate and you do not tolerate behavior that runs counter to the core values. See *Core Values* (Part 3.3.1), *Empowerment* (Part 3.4.1), and "Aligned Hiring" in *Strategic Management* (Part 3.5.2).

- **SIMPLIFICATION:** Overcoming challenges and taking advantage of opportunities depends on your ability to isolate and articulate the situation. You rely on many SMEs and know how to weigh their various points of view. See *Leadership Templates & Initiative* (Part 2.2) and *Simplify* (Part 3.6.2).

- **STRATEGIC ALIGNMENT – PLANNING:** Since you are not in the day-to-day, your strategic management routines are how you connect with your organization. You are especially active in strategic planning and business reviews. See *Strategic Alignment* (Part 3.4.2) and *Strategic Management* (Part 3.5.2).

In all of these roles, the strategic pause will be a part of your success. It is how you lead in the moment. I could list more than three ESA principles and methods for each role, though those listed will have the most impact.

4.3 Real-world Leadership Evolution

Leadership is a process, an evolution, not a destination. The "Real-world Leadership Evolution" leadership template shows leadership growth through the successive integration of ESA principles and methods outside of the classroom. There are ten steps in this leadership template. While some of names of the steps do not perfectly match the ESA *Principles* and *Methods*, the connection is clear.

Step		Level
10. Strategic Management Build a Distributed System, Build Leaders	**Leader**	Strategic Management
9. Simplify, Be Transparent Syntax & Semantics, On Message		
8. Strategic Alignment Vision & Objectives, Cascade Objectives		
7. Business Acumen Financials, Utilization, Pipeline, Legal		
6. People Management Meaningful 1-1s, Aligned Hiring	**Manager**	People Management
5. Empowerment Max Strengths & Min Weaknesses, Core Values		
4. Team Organization Team Workflow, Status		
3. Introspection Core Strengths, Personal Value Proposition	**Individual**	Productivity
2. Personal Organization Build an External Mind, Isolate Top Priorities		
1. Strategic Pause Situation Management, Be Cool & Composed		
0. Reactive Emotion in control		

The "Real-world Leadership Evolution" leadership template has three parts that are a simplified role evolution. Steps 1–3 are for the individual, with a focus on productivity. Steps 4–6 are for the manager, with a focus on people management. Steps 7–10 are for the leader, with a focus on strategic management.

0. **REACTIVE:** This is ground zero, the most extreme starting point. You are driven by instinct. Emotion is in control. See *The Strategic Pause* (Part 2).

1. **STRATEGIC PAUSE:** You seek more control over your day and your reactions. You discover that situation management gives you that control and enables composure. Practicing the strategic pause is the hub of your behavioral model from here on out. See *The Strategic Pause* (Part 2).

2. **PERSONAL ORGANIZATION:** You keep track of your work and set priorities. You build your first official personal organization system, which will adapt as you grow and your circumstances change. See *Personal Organization* (3.3.2).

3. **INTROSPECTION:** You realize that there are innate strengths driving your success. You strive to leverage those core strengths more and more. You see that introspection is far more than knowing the answers to the interview questions. See *Empowerment* (Part 3.4.1).

4. **TEAM ORGANIZATION:** You earn a promotion to management. Your first tasks as a manager are establishing the team's workflow, setting priorities, and providing status to those outside of your team. See *Personal Organization* (Part 3.3.2) and *Strategic Management* (Part 3.5.2).

5. **EMPOWERMENT:** You view your job as maximizing the strengths and minimizing the weaknesses of your team. You begin to understand that there are common core values and strengths across your best team members. See *Core Values* (Part 3.3.1) and *Empowerment* (Part 3.4.1).

6. **PEOPLE MANAGEMENT:** You begin to see management as building a system versus being dependent on individuals. You realize that it is much more than just hiring smart people. It is being committed to the routines that help your team members become subject matter experts and leaders. You make empowerment real via "Meaningful One-on-Ones" and "Aligned Hiring." See *Empowerment* (Part 3.4.1) and *Strategic Management* (Part 3.5.2).

7. **BUSINESS ACUMEN:** You are now responsible for long-term objectives. You need to understand what drives the business so that you can incorporate this knowledge into your planning and decision-making. See *Strategic Alignment* (Part 3.4.2) and *Strategic Management* (Part 3.5.2).

8. **STRATEGIC ALIGNMENT:** You understand the power of setting and cascading vivid objectives. You strive to align those objectives with the metrics that drive the business. See *Strategic Alignment* (Part 3.4.2).

9. **SIMPLIFY, BE TRANSPARENT:** As your responsibility grows, you see the increasing difficulty of isolating what is most important. You know that all information is not created equal. You are on message with the insights that matter. See *Simplify* (Part 3.6.2) and *Be Transparent* (Part 3.6.3).

10. **STRATEGIC MANAGEMENT:** You strive to leverage your team's minds and hands by building a distributed system. You view your routines as indispensable. Your strategic management system builds leaders and enables innovation. See *Strategic Management* (Part 3.5.2).

Since leadership evolution is a process of continuous improvement that does not always follow a straight course, expect to revisit previously covered steps to better align the principles and methods to your responsibilities and circumstances.

If you choose any of these leadership templates to guide the growth of your personal leadership model, use the "Evolution via Red, Yellow, Green" approach that we covered in *Leadership Model Evolution* (Part 3.1).

You now have four paths through ESA's content. In Part 3, you have the ESA leadership model itself. The path is walking through "Classroom Leadership Evolution" and is summarized in "ESA as Guardrails." You also have three alternative paths. "Satisfaction via Overlap" is a very simplified construct best suited for those early in their careers. "Role Evolution" lays out five career milestones and what is needed to reach and be successful at each milestone. "Real-world Leadership Evolution" walks you through the skills needed as you incrementally increase your responsibility.

The "Real-world Leadership Evolution" mimics my personal leadership journey. My hope is that one or all of these paths will aid in your internalization of ESA's principles and methods and accelerate the development of your own personal leadership model.

PART 5:

Closing Thoughts

5.1 Leading in the "New Normal"

The 2020 COVID-19 pandemic ushered in working in a "new normal." How is leadership different in this new normal? *Strategic Pause* contains the answer: leadership is leadership. The only change will be which principles or methods to emphasize and adapt in these new circumstances.

I simplify the new normal as full-time remote working on distributed teams.

Remote Working

Leading a remote and distributed team means that you emphasize the communication routines within strategic management.

1. **REGULAR ONE-ON-ONES:** If there was ever a time to not reschedule or cancel one-on-ones, this is the time. They are the primary connection between associate and manager. In addition to providing updates and feedback, strive to listen at least two-thirds of the time. Make sure your team member feels as though they are being heard.

2. **TEAM MEETINGS:** Team meetings are your primary mechanism for building community. If video is an option, use it. When people are on video, they are less likely to multi-task and more likely to be fully present. This includes you. Record the meetings for team members who cannot attend.

3. **VIVID AND CASCADED OBJECTIVES:** If each team member knows how they and their teammates impact the big picture; they will feel like a team. Your team will feel like they are in this together.

By the way, remote working was also a part of the old "new normal" that we were already adjusting to as companies became more global and remote. The pandemic accelerated the trend.

Replacing the Watercooler

The informal and serendipitous interactions of being in the office are gone with remote work. As the team's leader, you should strive to replace them in some form. And, like informal interactions, some should feel spontaneous. Use messaging and texting for quick check-ins or to offer words of encouragement. Host a contest to see who can display the most team spirit in their customized video meeting background. Reinforce the distributed system by referring questions to other team members who are in the know, even though you already know the answer. This will increase the support network of each member of the team. Do not be afraid to experiment. Even if a particular idea does not work, your team will appreciate the effort.

5.2 Make It Your Own

Throughout *Strategic Pause*, I have been consistent with this concept. As you leverage ESA to build your personal leadership model, you must make it your own. If you execute my leadership model, you will get results, but they may not be sustainable results. You will be running my system and not yours. You need to articulate and understand the *Principles* and *Methods* in your own words. You should strive to populate the *Differentiators* with the principles and methods that reflect who you are. Doing so internalizes and puts your signature on your personal leadership model. It is your leadership style.

The ESA leadership model provides guardrails for the "what" and the "how" of leadership. Making it your own is adding the "who." The who is you. Add your own emphasis on the principles, methods, and differentiators that mean the most to you. Continue to evolve your personal leadership model and grow as a leader. Always remember that leadership is a process, not a destination.

5.3 Fulfilling Potential

Practicing strategic pauses and building your personal leadership model makes you a better leader of both yourself and your team. With ESA, you isolate core strengths and align to objectives. You do what you do best: deliver sustainable results and impact the big picture. There is a good chance that you are fulfilling both your own potential and that of your team.

Fulfilling your potential means a number of things. You are independent. You give more than you receive. You make the most of your talents and make progress toward something bigger. As a result, I believe that you will be more satisfied and happier. My purpose for sharing ESA is driven by a desire to help you fulfill your potential and be happy.

5.4 Accelerating Human Evolution

Human evolution has a leading edge which represents the height of human advancement. This includes finding cures for diseases, connecting the people of the world through technology, and making more efficient use of the earth's resources. Human advancement is not limited to the technical realm. It includes a broader understanding and use of distributed systems, recognition of human rights across the globe, and wider availability of education to all populations. Human advancement has a broad definition that is influenced by broad populations, including you and your team. Human evolution is getting an increasing percentage of the population closer to that leading edge so they can push it out even farther. The sooner people discover their core strengths and learn how to align to bigger objectives, the sooner they will be able to influence the leading edge of human evolution.

Practicing strategic pauses and building your personal leadership model using ESA as your guardrails enables you and your team to fulfill your potential. You will climb the evolution curve much more quickly than without them. In this way, believe it or not, you are accelerating human evolution. You are playing your part.

PART 6:

Artifacts

For reference, below are the four artifacts I anticipate that you will continually refer to. We have leveraged them in building out ESA and explaining leadership evolution.

6.1 The ESA Leadership Model

ESA

"Know how you impact the big picture"

	Foundation (Operational)	Present (Tactical)	Future (Strategic)
Principles	**Core Values** • Mutual Respect • Work Ethic • Responsibility • Integrity • Credibility	**Empowerment (E)** • Max Strengths, Min Weaknesses • "Do what you do best every day"	**Strategic Alignment (SA)** • Set Vivid Vision & Objectives • Cascade Vision & Objectives – Create a "line of sight"
Methods	**Personal Organization** • Build an External Mind • Be Ready: Status, • Run Scenarios • The Power of Little Habits	**The Strategic Pause** • Be Cool & Composed • Take Initiative & • Challenge the BAU • Align to Core & Objectives	**Strategic Management** • Build a Distributed System • NOT Optional
Differentiators	**Be a Positive Force** • Enthusiasm, Optimism, Humor • View as an Opportunity or a Challenge	**Simplify** • Syntax & Semantics • Min Admin, Max Value	**Be Transparent** • On Message • Manage to One Reality

6.2 **Strategic Management**

Strategic Management

Planning

Core Values	Core Strengths, Value Proposition
Objectives	Vision
Strategic Planning	Objectives Cascade
Business Review	

Management

Status & Alignment	Admin (Fins, Util, Pipeline, Legal)
Meaningful 1-1s	Aligned Hiring
Team Meetings	Anonymous Feedback
Aligned Recognition	Intelligence Sharing

Measurement

Scorecard	Client Survey
Team Engagement Assessment	Objectives Grade Out

6.3 ESA as Guardrails

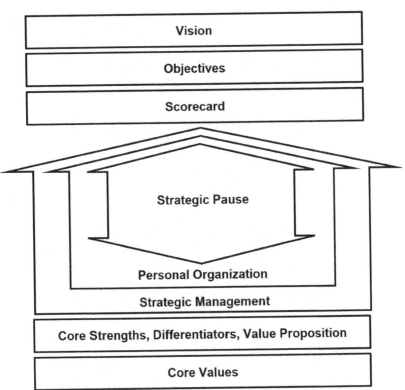

6.4 **Real-world Leadership Evolution**

10. **Strategic Management** Build a Distributed System, Build Leaders	**Leader**	**Strategic Management**
9. **Simplify, Be Transparent** Syntax & Semantics, On Message		
8. **Strategic Alignment** Vision & Objectives, Cascade Objectives		
7. **Business Acumen** Financials, Utilization, Pipeline, Legal		
6. **People Management** Meaningful 1-1s, Aligned Hiring	**Manager**	**People Management**
5. **Empowerment** Max Strengths & Min Weaknesses, Core Values		
4. **Team Organization** Team Workflow, Status		
3. **Introspection** Core Strengths, Personal Value Proposition	**Individual**	**Productivity**
2. **Personal Organization** Build an External Mind, Isolate Top Priorities		
1. **Strategic Pause** Situation Management, Be Cool & Composed		

0. **Reactive**
Emotion in control

Acknowledgments

First, I need to thank my editor and friend, Robin Gullicksen. She retaught me how to write: to challenge my assumptions, check my use of buzzwords, and always think of my audience first. Robin's deep commitment to my leadership book means it is also her leadership book.

Thank you to my beta readers: Stacie Lang, Ben Lohnes, and Joe Lidoski. Their feedback was a source of encouragement and led to important improvements of my passion project.

I would like to thank all of my managers. I learned something from each and every one of them. As you read in the book, Brad Emerson and Brad Neuenhaus had a particularly meaningful impact on me.

My friends—Steve Morgenstern, Joe Lidoski, Mike Hurley, Dwight Emery, Ilya Ehrlich, Rich Murphy, Satish Hariharan, Jon Casciari, and Hans Jackson—deserve special thanks for being my sounding boards. Their input has been instrumental in my leadership model's evolution over the years.

I am always thankful to my mom and dad, Randi and Warren Graumann. I am who I am because of the example they set. My learning experiences shared in the book are just the tip of the iceberg. I also want to thank my in-laws, Dot and Ron Plante, who are a constant source of support.

Finally, I must thank my daughters, Emily and Abby, and my wife, Laurie. My daughters inspire me every day. I could not be prouder of who they have grown to be. In many ways, I wrote this book for them. They have always been patient listening to my monologues on leadership and personal productivity. My wife, Laurie, is my rock and my best friend. Her candid and objective perspectives have been critical to my growth. Her unconditional support is my foundation.

Leadership Template Index

No Big Thinking Sunday Night & Monday Morning (Leadership Template) 43

Can vs. Can't Control (Leadership Template) 45

Know When Good Enough is Good Enough (Leadership Template) 46

Effective over Efficient (Leadership Template) 48

The Skills Pie (Leadership Template) 55

Consistent Expectation Setting (Leadership Template) 69

How to Be a Good Person (Leadership Template) 73

Personal Organization System Framework (Leadership Template) 77

Choose Important over Urgent (Leadership Template) 80

Creating a Win-Win by Reframing Priorities (Leadership Template) 81

Organized at the Appropriate Level (Leadership Template) 82

Beware of False Obligations (Leadership Template) 83

Ten-minute Rule (Leadership Template) 88

Know Your Resets (Leadership Template) 95

Your Point of Diminishing Returns (Leadership Template) 96

Situational People Management (Leadership Template) 104

Best Practices + 1 (Leadership Template) 114

Cascade as Lead Measures (Leadership Template) 116

Leverage Minds and Hands (Leadership Template) 122

Lead Them to Their Own Conclusion (Leadership Template) 125

Balance Process and Results (Leadership Template) 126

Strategic Procrastination (Leadership Template) 127

Top-down and Bottom-up Strategy (Leadership Template) 143

Trend Progression Strategy (Leadership Template) 144

Beware of Compliance (Leadership Template) 160

Connect Status with Rate of Change (Leadership Template) 175

Transparency in Projects (Leadership Template) 178

Leadership Examples Index

Situation Management in my Childhood (Leadership Example) 35

The Unsent Angry Email (Leadership Example) 36

Staying Composed in a Cube Farm (Leadership Example) 37

Witnessing my Mom's Composure (Leadership Example) 38

Efficient Errands (Leadership Example) 44

The Secure Data Hub & PCI Compliance (Leadership Example) 47

Writing My Leadership Book (Leadership Example) 47

Ignoring My Gut and the Project Manager (Leadership Example) 72

Ready for Due Diligence (Leadership Example) 85

Big Automotive Client and Scalable Growth (Leadership Example) 86

Audit Ready (Leadership Example) 87

Debating on Your Home Field (Leadership Example) 96

A Programmer Should Program (Leadership Example) 98

The Account Manager with Sales Skills (Leadership Example) 99

Scalability through Empowerment (Leadership Example) 100

The Accessible Executive (Leadership Example) 100

Breaking into Identification Services (Leadership Example) 109

The Power of YouTube (Leadership Example) 112

Vivid Vision and Objectives (Leadership Example) 113

100% Client Advocacy (Leadership Example) 114

The Efficiency Lunch (Leadership Example) 124

The Strategic Pause and War (Leadership Example) 128

Distributed Warfare (Leadership Example) 135

Value Propositions (Leadership Example) 139

Loyalty Objectives and Vision (Leadership Example) 141

What is left in the tank? (Leadership Example) 155

Be a Positive Force and Parenting (Leadership Example) 169

Rising through the Breach (Leadership Example) 169

The Delayed Proposal Win (Leadership Example) 179

About the Author

Don Graumann is a high-performance executive and leadership coach whose teams are known for delivering sustainable results. He has worked in insight-driven marketing for almost 30 years. His purpose is helping individuals and teams fulfill their potential. Don has a BS in Mathematics from Bates College and an MBA from Boston College. His math and programming roots taught him the value of focusing on "first principles," a fundamental concept which he applies to everything in his life, including leadership and personal productivity. Don lives in Massachusetts with his wife, twin daughters, and two dogs.

StrategicPause.com (Leadership Blog)

www.linkedin.com/in/dongraumann/ (LinkedIn)

@DonThinks (Twitter)

Made in the USA
Monee, IL
27 January 2021

58844415R00128